CANADIAN CONCEPTS

Second Edition

Lynda Berish

Sandra Thibaudeau

Collège Marie-Victorin

Canadian Cataloguing in Publication Data

Berish, Lynda, date
  Canadian concepts 4

2nd ed.
ISBN 978-0-13-591710-7

1. English language—Textbooks for second language learners.*
2. English Language—Grammar.   3. English language—
Problems, exercises, etc.   I. Thibaudeau, Sandra, date.   II. Title.

PE1128.B473 1997   428.2'4   C96-931829-4

Allyn and Bacon, Inc., Needham Heights, Massachusetts
Prentice-Hall, Inc., Upper Saddle River, New Jersey
Prentice-Hall International (UK) Limited, London
Prentice-Hall of Australia, Pty., Ltd., Sydney
Prentice-Hall Hispanoamericana, S. A., Mexico
Prentice-Hall of India Private Limited, New Delhi
Prentice-Hall of Japan, Inc., Tokyo
Prentice-Hall of Southeast Asia (PTE) Ltd., Singapore
Simon & Schuster Asia Private Limited, Singapore
Editora Prentice-Hall do Brasil Ltda., Rio de Janeiro

ISBN 978-0-13-591710-7

Acquisitions editor: Dominique Roberge
Developmental editor: Marta Tomins
Production editor: Elynor Kagan
Editorial assistant: Rita Self
Production coordinator: Sharon Houston
Design: Monica Kompter
Layout: Joseph Chin
Text illustrations: Allan and Deborah Drew-Brook Cormack
Unit opening illlustrations: Carole Giguère
Cover Image: Dave Reede/First Light. Canola Grain Elevator, Holland, Manitoba

Printed and bound in Canada

7   8   9   M   18   17   16   15

To Millicent and Max Goldman for their support
in many ways over the years.

CONTENTS

LISTENING ACTIVITIES	VIDEO ACTIVITIES
1. Old Friends	1. The Yellow Pages (3:10 minutes)
2. Doing What We Can	
3. Where Should We Eat?	2. Having a Snack (1:28 minutes)
4. Getting in Shape	
5. Planning a Vacation	3. Spring Excuses (1:31 minutes)

		TOPICS	GRAMMAR
6	**If You Get Hurt** Page 71	**The human body** Accidents and injuries At the orthopedic clinic	Passive Voice
7	**Where Does the Time Go?** Page 87	**Daily activities** Time management Being on time Waiting	"How much"/"How many"
8	**It's All in the Family** Page 99	**Marriage and divorce** Arranged marriages Family roles	Conditional I
9	**Where Does Your Money Go?** Page 111	**Banking** Using a banking machine Money terms Making money Sweepstakes	Present Perfect Aspect for Duration of Time Affirmative, Negative Questions
10	**Getting a Job** Page 123	**Looking for a job** The job interview	"Have to"/"Don't have to"/ "Must not"

TO THE TEACHER

The *Canadian Concepts* Series

The new edition of the popular *Canadian Concepts* series retains the Canadian focus designed to help students feel at home and integrate into the community. In the new edition, exercises and activities have been graded and, in some cases, refocussed to provide a careful build-up of skills throughout the series. *Canadian Concepts 1* is paced to accommodate the needs of post-literacy students, while *Canadian Concepts 2* moves ahead to introduce new vocabulary and grammatical structures at a faster pace. *Canadian Concepts 3* provides a richer field of vocabulary and a greater degree of challenge while reinforcing the themes of the lower levels. *Canadian Concepts 4, 5,* and *6* integrate video materials on Canadian themes.

The *Canadian Concepts* series uses a communicative approach. The method offers productive strategies for language learning based on student-centred interaction. Many new activities, games, and opportunities for speaking have been incorporated into the series to encourage maximum student participation in classroom activities. The pedagogical model presents students with challenging listening or reading input, leading them through pre-activities and strategies that make the input comprehensible. In addition to these fluency-building activities, dictation, grammar, spelling, and vocabulary work focus on improving students' accuracy.

Canadian Concepts 4

Canadian Concepts 4 focuses on interesting and practical topics that prepare students for life in Canada. A rich variety of activities gives students ample opportunity to interact and exchange information and ideas. Community Contact Tasks give students the opportunity to practise their English in real-life situations outside the classroom. Clear illustrations, a lively format, and a wide variety of activities keep students interested and involved

Canadian Concepts 4 is made up of ten self-contained thematic units. Core activities focus on reading, listening, and viewing videos. Reading texts may be adapted from newspaper articles or feature easily accessible articles. Listening activities include dialogues and interviews. Video activities provide a dynamic new element to the listening program. Video segments ranging from 2 to 7 minutes are taken from CBC news programs such as *Marketplace, Venture,* and *Country Canada.* While the topics are interesting, relevant, and fun, they are also carefully chosen to ensure they are accessible to students at this level. The video activities give students an opportunity to listen for information delivered in authentic English.

Throughout the units, students are asked to work on challenging material, using visuals and a variety of activities as support. New language is reviewed and expanded upon in many different ways, from games and puzzles to stimulating discussion topics. Grammar and writing activities provide ample opportunity for practice and expression.

Each unit concludes with a series of problem-solving activities that are related to the topic. Many of these activities involve discussions about social and cultural issues, and deal with problems students might encounter in a new country.

Students are motivated to use their new skills in the real world through Community Contact Tasks provided at the end of the book.

Teachers and students will appreciate the simple format and lively appearance of the materials, with clear illustrations that lend valuable visual support. They will also enjoy browsing through Canadian Capsules that provide background information on Canada. Worksheets to accompany many of the activities in *Canadian Concepts 4* are provided in the Teacher's Manual and Resource Package, with permission to photocopy.

KEY TO SYMBOLS

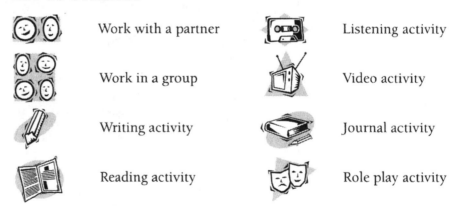

	Work with a partner		Listening activity
	Work in a group		Video activity
	Writing activity		Journal activity
	Reading activity		Role play activity

Teacher's Manual and Resource Package

A fun-packed Teacher's Manual and Resource Package provides myriad suggestions for expanding activities in the student book and for getting the most out of activities. It has many pages that can be photocopied, as well as an answer key and tape scripts.

At the End of the Course

Students who successfully complete this level will be ready for *Canadian Concepts 5*, which features stimulating themes for discussion and interaction, authentic newspaper and magazine articles, more CBC videos, and lively interviews.

UNIT 1

FINDING YOUR WAY

MEETING AND GREETING

A Work in a group. Discuss these questions.

1. Where do you come from?
   (Which country and city?)

2. What language or languages
   do you speak?

3. What is your name and does it
   have a meaning? (Spell your
   name for your partners, and
   write each other's names.)

4. What do people do when they
   meet in your culture? (Do they
   shake hands, bow, kiss, etc.?)

5. What do two people say when they meet in your culture? (Say the
   words in **your** language and then translate the exact meaning.)

6. What subjects are usual for conversation in your culture when people
   meet for the first time?

B   Which subjects do people **not** talk about when they meet for the first time in Canada?

1.   the weather

2.   their jobs

3.   religion

4.   marital status

5.   clothes and fashion

6.   their ages

7.   sports results

8.   cars

9.   their families

10.   their salaries

11.   their level of education

12.   politics

13.   items in the news

14.   food and restaurants

15.   their health

16.   their pets

OLD FRIENDS

LISTENING ACTIVITY 1

A   Read the questions aloud with a partner.

B   Listen and answer the questions.

1.   How long ago did Peter and Marco work together?

2.   What is Marco's big news?

3.   Where did Marco and Sandra meet?

4.   What is Sandra doing at the moment?

5.   What does Sandra remember hearing about Peter?

6.   Whose idea was it to get rid of Peter's car?

7.   When does Sandra suggest they get together?

8.   Where does Marco work?

9.   Why does Sandra suggest that Peter call tomorrow?

10.   What does Peter look forward to?

Turn to page 11 for Exercise C.

CANADIAN CAPSULES

Some Canadians shake hands when they greet each other. Other Canadians kiss each other on the cheek, or hug quickly to greet each other.

SAME AND DIFFERENT

A Work with a partner. Discuss these questions.

1. How long have you lived here?

2. Do you come from a big city or a smaller town?

3. Did you live in another city in Canada before you came here?

4. Have you noticed any differences between people's behaviour here and in other places you have lived?

B Work in a group. Compare these customs with customs in your culture. Make a chart similar to the one below. Write **S** (same) or **D** (different) for you and your partner. If your answer is **D**, discuss the custom in your culture.

1. People always line up at bus stops.

2. There are wastebaskets for litter in public places.

3. Pedestrians don't cross the street against a red light.

4. Fathers, as well as mothers, often carry babies.

5. Most people walk very quickly along the sidewalk.

6. Friends kiss each other on the cheek when they meet.

7. Many people read books or magazines in the subway.

8. Someone in the street may ask you for spare change.

9. Passengers enter the bus by the front door.

10. Passengers exit the bus by the back door.

11. Women work as bus drivers and police officers.

12. It is easy to find a public telephone.

	Me	Partner
1.		
2.		
3.		
4.		
5.		
6.		

XUAN'S DIARY

A   Read Xuan's diary and discuss answers to the questions **orally**.

Since my airplane landed at Vancouver International Airport, I have had a hard time trying to understand this new culture. From the first moment, everything seemed unfamiliar. My brother and his wife met me at the airport. There were so many big cars on the road when we drove to their home. There were so many bright lights in the city and such strange foods in the stores. The biggest problem was changing from my Oriental ways to new western ways. Not many people understand what it is like to change cultures.

For my first month in Canada, I was waiting for language classes to start. I didn't want to leave the house at all. Mostly I watched TV, or when no one was home, I cried. I also slept a lot. My brother and sister-in-law were at work all day. I didn't have a family member or friend to talk to. I didn't know who my neighbours were. At home there was always someone to talk to. Here there was no one. I especially missed my mother and my sister. At home in Shanghai we always slept together in the same bed. Here my sister-in-law said I should get used to my own room. I felt very lonely and confused.

When I started school, I found that it was different too. In China, when the teacher asked a question, you had to stand up to answer it. Here, when the teacher asked my name, I stood up to answer and everyone in the class laughed. I felt very embarrassed. Here people call the teacher by her first name, even if the teacher is old. My teacher said her name was Jan so I called her Teacher Jan. Again the other students laughed. I felt my face get red.

Now I am beginning to understand life here better. I know that the students in my class were laughing because they had made the same mistakes when they came. I am beginning to make friends with students in the class and I don't feel so lonely. I even met another girl from China. On Saturday we are going to go shopping in Chinatown. Maybe life in Canada will be OK after all.

1. Who met Xuan at the airport?

2. Which things seemed unfamiliar to her? (Name three.)

3. What was the biggest difficulty she faced?

4. What symptoms of culture shock did Xuan experience? (Name three.)

5. Why was she so lonely? (Give two reasons.)

6. How were sleeping arrangements in Canada different from sleeping arrangements in China?

7. What was the first mistake Xuan made in her English class?

8. What was the second mistake she made at school?

9. What did she realize about the other students in her class?

10. What plan makes her feel better about life in Canada?

B Read Xuan's diary again and answer the questions in writing. Use your notebook.

Simple Past Tense

The simple past tense describes actions or states that were completed in past time.

In the affirmative, the simple past tense can have regular or irregular verb forms. For the regular form add **ed** to the base form of the verb. For common irregular past tense (affirmative) forms see Appendix 2, page 149.

A Work in pairs. Copy and complete the chart of regular and irregular verb forms below.

1.	see	_____	9. make	_____
2.	_____	ran	10. _____	said
3.	meet	_____	11. invite	_____
4.	work	_____	12. write	_____
5.	_____	told	13. _____	went
6.	think	_____	14. talk	_____
7.	_____	got	15. _____	was/were
8.	have/has	_____		

B   Choose the verbs that complete the sentences below. Use the **simple past tense**.

**eat   find   study   go   meet   run   write   think   speak
come   tell   talk   sit   see   make**

1.   Ling-Ling _____ to Canada from China last year.

2.   Pedro _____ home to Mexico for a visit at Christmas.

3.   Sylvie _____ computer science when she was at college.

4.   Nikos _____ a letter to his brother after he found work.

5.   The teacher _____ his lunch with the students yesterday.

6.   My friends and I _____ a really good movie on the weekend.

7.   Julie _____ her friend Keiko at the airport this morning.

8.   When she first arrived, Ida _____ people were very friendly.

9.   Nobody _____ us that we couldn't smoke in the classroom.

10.   This morning my neighbour _____ to catch the bus.

11.   The two friends _____ on the phone all evening yesterday.

12.   The new students _____ the classroom easily the first day.

13.   Most people _____ friends quickly in the English class.

14.   Ana and Victor _____ at the same table at lunch today.

15.   Burhan _____ softly when he answered questions in class.

Simple Past Tense: Negative

In the **negative** form of the simple past, add **did + not** between the subject and the base form of the main verb.

> James **went** home early.   James **did not go** home early.

The contraction of **did not** is **didn't**.

> James **didn't go** home early.

   Change the sentences to the negative. Use the contraction. Write in your notebook.

1.   We **shook** hands with all the people we met at the party.

2.   Min Hee **ate** oysters when we went to the restaurant last night.

3.   Pierre and Marc **talked** in French during class this morning.

4.   Michiko **stood** in line for the bus for a long time yesterday.

5.   Franco **took** an English course when he was in London.

6. They **felt** nervous when they met the new people in the class.

7. Our friends **had** a good time on their vacation last month.

8. We **visited** our cousins when we were at home last year.

9. Geraldo **told** his classmates that he was getting married.

10. Annie **said** that she planned to go to Madrid on vacation.

B   Which sentences are wrong? Correct the errors.

1. Mario **didn't felt** nervous when the teacher asked for the answer.

2. Michiko **didn't made** any mistakes in her English exam yesterday.

3. The hostess **didn't introduced** the guests to each other.

4. Our friends **didn't come** by train last weekend.

5. Han Lim **didn't saw** the movie at the campus theatre.

6. The teacher **didn't gives** us any homework yesterday.

7. We **didn't understood** the instructions we saw on the package.

8. Maria **didn't speak** English very well when we first met.

9. I **didn't knew** many people's names at the party last night.

10. Gaby **didn't attend** class yesterday because she was sick.

Simple Past Tense: Questions

For the question form of the simple past, put **did** before the subject + the base form of the main verb.

> **Did** you **come** by train?

A   Change the statements into questions.

1. He enjoyed the movie that he saw last night.

2. They said that the play was interesting.

3. Everyone at the party spoke English well.

4. Henri tried to speak Spanish to the visitors.

5. The group went to Ottawa by train last weekend.

6. Anita shook Claudia Schiffer's hand at the party.

7. My sister ran for the bus this morning.

8. They talked about their English course.

9. Hiroshi saw his cousin at the train station.

10. Karen waved goodbye from the window of the train.

B   Match the questions and the answers.

1. **Where** did you go yesterday?
2. **How** did you travel to Toronto?
3. **When** did you hear that information?
4. **What** did they see during their holiday?
5. **Why** did everyone wear raincoats on the boat?
6. **Who** did you meet when you were at the beach?
7. **How** did they find out our names?
8. **When** did the group arrive at the hotel?
9. **Who** did you tell about our plans?
10. **What** did the teacher do first in the class?

a)   I didn't meet anyone while I was there.

b)   They saw Niagara Falls from a passenger boat.

c)   We wore them because it was wet on the boat.

d)   We went to the swimming pool.

e)   I didn't tell anyone about our plans.

f)   She introduced all the students to each other.

g)   They arrived there after dinner yesterday.

h)   We went there by train.

i)   They asked Mario what we were called.

j)   I heard it on the radio yesterday.

JOURNAL

Write about your first impressions of the city you are in now and the culture of the people who live here.

CANADIAN CAPSULES

The custom of shaking hands probably began when strangers were possible enemies. Both people opened their hands to show they were not armed. Then they shook hands to show that they wanted to be friends.

YELLOW PAGES

CBC

VIDEO ACTIVITY 1

A   Work in a group and answer these questions.

1. When was the last time you looked in the Yellow Pages directory?

2. How many times a year do you estimate that you look in the Yellow Pages directory?

3. What are some services you can find out about in the Yellow Pages directory? Make a list.

4. What attracts you to particular ads in the Yellow Pages directory?

B   Read the questions below **aloud** with a partner.

C   Watch the video and answer the questions. Use the worksheet.

1. What is Tele-Direct?

2. How many times a year does the average consumer look in the Yellow Pages directory?

3. What three things work in an ad?

4. What do ads for plumbers often show?

5. What two things do lawyers want to show us?

6. How many **A**s did Robertson use in his ad?

7. What is public reaction to using a lot of **A**s?

8. Who is the winner for using the most **A**s?

9. What types of businesses often mention how long they have been in business? (Name three.)

10. How long do people say a company should be in business before they brag about it?

PROBLEM SOLVING

What Would You Do?

A Work in a group. Discuss what you would do in each of these situations:

1. You find yourself at a party where the only people you know are the host and hostess. What is the best thing to do?

   a) Make an excuse about not feeling well and go home.
   b) Ask the host or hostess to introduce you to people.
   c) Approach a group you don't know and introduce yourself.
   d) Go up to someone who is alone and start a conversation.

2. You are invited to a friend's house for dinner at 6:30. At 6:15 you are on a bus in a traffic jam and you realize you will be at least 40 minutes late. What would you do?

   a) Stay on the bus and not worry about it too much.
   b) Get off the bus and telephone to say you will be late.
   c) Get off the bus and try to find a taxi to arrive faster.
   d) Other. (Explain.)

3. About an hour before your dinner party, a guest calls to ask if you would mind if he brought along a friend who is visiting. You don't think you have enough food for an extra person. How would you handle the situation?

   a) Tell the guest he can't bring his friend, but invite them both to come another time.
   b) Say you aren't really hungry (so there will be enough food).
   c) Ask the guest to stop and pick up some extra food on the way.
   d) Rush out and buy some extra food that is already prepared.

4. You arrive for dinner at a new friend's house and realize that everyone has brought something for the meal. You suddenly understand what the hostess meant by a pot-luck dinner. What would you do?

   a) Excuse yourself and go out to get something to contribute.
   b) Say you aren't very hungry and don't eat anything.
   c) Explain that you didn't understand and ask the hostess for advice.
   d) Explain the misunderstanding and then forget about it.

B Customs for entertaining are different in different cultures. In your culture:

a) How are invitations given?

b) Who is usually invited?

c) Do people arrive on time?

d) How do people know when to leave?

Have you noticed any strange or confusing customs here? Discuss them in your group.

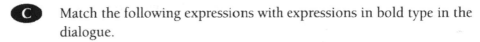

OLD FRIENDS

LISTENING ACTIVITY 1

C Match the following expressions with expressions in bold type in the dialogue.

1. Why?

2. invite you to our house

3. been doing with your life

4. cheaper to operate (a car)

5. We haven't met for a long time.

6. are free at that time

7. exchange news about the past

8. meet you

9. the most important event

10. I no longer have it/do it

D Practise the dialogue in a group of three.

Peter: Hey, Marco. **Long time no see**. How are you these days?

Marco: Fine Peter. Hey, it's nice to **run into you**. How long has it been since we worked on that project?

Peter: At least three years. So what have you **been up to**?

Marco: Well **the big news** is I'm married. I'd like you to meet my wife Sandra. Sandra, Peter and I worked together in that office at the printers just after we graduated.

Peter: Pleased to meet you, Sandra. Congratulations to both of you.

Marco: Sandra and I met in Vancouver two years ago when I was working out there. Sandra is looking for work here at the moment.

Sandra: Nice to meet you too, Peter. Marco's told me a lot about you. You were the guy with the flashy car, weren't you?

Peter: Oh yeah. I loved that car. **It's a thing of the past** now.

Sandra: Oh, **how come**?

Marco: Yeah Peter. I thought you would never get rid of that car.

Peter: Well, you know how it is. I got married last year too. It wasn't exactly a family car. Emily, that's my wife, preferred something **a little easier on the gas**.

Sandra: Well, congratulations to both of you too, Marco. We'd love to meet your wife. If you are free next Saturday, we'd love **to have you over**.

Marco: Why don't you check with Emily, Peter? Here is our address and telephone number. I operate a small business out of the basement. We would be very happy if you and Emily **can make it** next Saturday.

Sandra: Yes, Peter, call us tomorrow to let us know if Saturday is OK. We'll look forward to seeing you.

Peter: I'll certainly call. It'll be great to **catch up on old times**.

TAKING CARE OF THE EARTH

IN YOUR HOME

A Complete the chart. You should have six groups of three words each.

**package can throw away container refill jar manufacture
glass get rid of wrapping cardboard bottle dump plastic
make recycle produce reuse**

1. refill	1. produce	1. can
2.	2.	2.
3.	3.	3.
1. package	1. glass	1. throw away
2.	2.	2.
3.	3.	3.

B   Look at the two pictures of kitchens. One family helps the environment in many ways. The other family doesn't do very much to help the environment.

Work in pairs. Make a list of ten things to help the environment that Family A does but Family B doesn't do. When you have finished, turn to page 26 to check your ideas.

Family A

Family B

CANADIAN CAPSULES

Look for this symbol on the products that you buy. It is the recycling symbol. It shows that an item can be recycled. The three arrows are for the different types of products that can be recycled: solids, liquids, and gases.

THE PACKAGING PROBLEM

A   Read the paragraph. Then close your book and write while the teacher dictates.

> One of the problems we face in Canada is that we produce too much garbage. Getting rid of garbage is the responsibility of city and provincial governments. They are thinking of different ways to solve the garbage problem. One province does not allow stores to sell soft-drink bottles that cannot be refilled. Another province puts a special tax on bottles that cannot be refilled.

B   Complete the paragraph with the words below.

bottles   packaging   boxes   aisle   plastic   cans   problem jars   styrofoam

Think about packaging in our modern supermarkets. As you walk down the __1__ you will notice that almost everything comes in some kind of package or container. Meat, fruit, and vegetables have cardboard or styrofoam under them and __2__ over them. Jam and peanut butter come in glass or plastic __3__, juice comes in plastic __4__, and soup comes in metal __5__. Rice comes in plastic bags or cardboard __6__. Eggs come in __7__ or cardboard. With so much __8__, it's no wonder we have a __9__ with garbage.

C   Work in groups. Look at the pictures of the food containers. What materials are used in the packaging? If you need help, use the listed words.

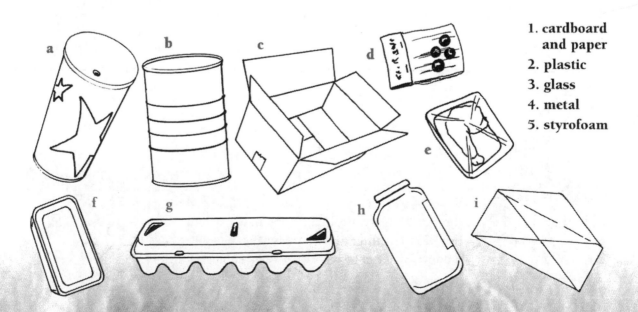

1. cardboard and paper
2. plastic
3. glass
4. metal
5. styrofoam

THE GARBAGE QUIZ

A   Work in a group. Discuss and choose the best answers.

1. Most of the garbage in Canada is in the form of:
   a) glass
   b) metal
   c) paper

2. Most of the garbage that is collected in Canada is:
   a) burned in incinerators
   b) dumped in a hole in the ground
   c) buried under the ground

3. The biggest problem with most garbage dumps is that they:
   a) smell bad
   b) look bad
   c) use too much land

4. It is bad to burn garbage because it:
   a) becomes too hot to handle
   b) puts harmful chemicals in the air
   c) has an unpleasant smell

5. The styrofoam thrown out daily in North America could make:
   a) five million coffee cups
   b) 17 million coffee cups
   c) 900 million coffee cups

6. Put these items in order by how many are thrown away each year, from most to least.
   a) plastic razors
   b) car tires
   c) plastic pens

7. If you throw a glass bottle away, how long does it take for it to disappear?
   a) one hundred years
   b) one and a half years
   c) one thousand years

8. Most aluminium is used to make:
    a) soft-drink containers
    b) doors and windows
    c) airplanes

9. The energy saved from recycling one aluminium can could:
    a) make another aluminium can
    b) operate a television for three hours
    c) operate a hair dryer for an hour

10. Each day, the newsprint used for newspapers in Canada uses up:
    a) 4000 trees
    b) 14 000 trees
    c) 40 000 trees

11. Half the plastic we throw away each year comes from:
    a) packaging
    b) shampoo bottles
    c) plastic razors

12. For every $10 you spend on food, the packaging costs:
    a) $0.50
    b) $1.00
    c) $1.50

B   Turn to page 27 and read to check your answers.

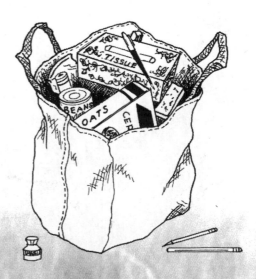

TOO MUCH GARBAGE

A   Read the text. Then answer the questions **orally** with a partner.

Too Much Garbage

What do a chocolate bar, a new plastic razor, and a new shirt have in common? They are all wrapped in layers of packaging. All this packaging goes into the garbage. If you dumped out the average Canadian's garbage from last year, it would fill up your living room, kitchen, bedroom, and most of the bathroom. You would find plastic bags, food scraps, old newspapers, junk mail, glass jars, batteries, medicines, and many other things.

Canada is a nation of consumers. This means that we buy a lot of products. Most of the products we buy are wrapped in paper, plastic, or styrofoam. After we buy the products, we throw away the wrapping. In addition, we throw away many of the products we buy after using them once or twice. The average Canadian household produces one tonne of garbage every year.

What happens to your garbage when you put it outside your door to be collected? Usually the garbage goes to a landfill site—a big field with a hole where we dump out garbage. As we keep adding more garbage to the hole, it becomes a mountain—a mountain of garbage. Now we have a problem: what can we do with all this garbage? Many landfill sites are closing because they are full. We will soon have nowhere to put our garbage.

A second problem is that all the garbage we produce is a waste of natural resources. Thousands of trees are cut down every day to make paper products and newsprint. Oil is used to make millions of plastic bags and food containers. Thousands of tonnes of aluminium are used to make cans for food and drinks. The energy used to make all these products could be used for more important things, such as heating our houses in winter.

A third problem is that when products are manufactured, chemicals are used, These chemicals are often released into the air as smoke during the manufacturing process. They pollute the air we breathe. In addition, some manufacturers dump the chemicals they no longer need into the rivers and oceans, or they dump them in the ground where they can get into our drinking water.

Fortunately, there are steps we can take to reduce our garbage. We can avoid excess packaging by choosing the products that have the least amount of packaging. We can use items more than once. We can recycle many items so they can be made into new products.

CANADIAN CAPSULES

Many cities in Canada have recycling programs. People are encouraged to separate their garbage into paper, glass, plastics, and metal. They put these items into recycling boxes, which are usually blue or green. Then the items are recycled and made into new products.

1. What do the three products mentioned in the first paragraph have in common?

2. How many rooms of the house would the average person's yearly garbage fill up?

3. Why is Canada called "a nation of consumers"?

4. What are the three most common wrapping products?

5. How many tonnes of garbage does a Canadian household produce annually?

6. What is a landfill site?

7. What problem do we have with landfill sites?

8. What three resources are used up to make packaging?

9. What is suggested as a more important use of energy than making packaging?

10. How do the chemicals used in manufacturing certain products get into the air?

11. How do some manufacturers get rid of chemicals they no longer need?

12. What are three steps we can take to reduce our garbage?

B   Write answers to the questions. Use your notebook.

GRAMMAR FOCUS Giving Advice Using "Should"

Use **should** to give advice or to express opinions. Use the negative form, **should not**, to advise against doing something. The contraction of **should not** is **shouldn't**.

Use **should** before the base form of the main verb.

A   Match the problem and the solution.

1. Empty bottles create pollution.

2. Unnecessary wrapping is used on food.

3. Supermarkets use too many plastic bags.

4. Companies dump toxic wastes.

5. Newsprint consumption leads to forest destruction.

6. Many products are disposable.

a) Pass legislation.

b) Buy food without wrapping.

c) Avoid buying them.

d) Refill them.

e) Bring bags to the store.

f) Recycle paper and plant trees.

B Use the information in Exercise A. Write sentences giving advice with should or shouldn't. Use your notebook.

> We should refill empty bottles.
>
> We shouldn't throw them away.

GRAMMAR FOCUS — Giving Advice Using "Must"

Use **must** to give strong or urgent advice or opinions. Use the negative form **must not** to strongly advise against doing something. The contraction of **must** is **mustn't**. Don't pronounce the first **t** in **mustn't**.

A Complete the sentences with **must** or **mustn't**.

1. The lake is polluted with toxic waste. People _____ drink the water.

2. We are running out of places to store our garbage. We _____ find solutions quickly.

3. Many cities now have recycling programs. We _____ forget to recycle our garbage.

4. Scientists warn that we are destroying the ozone layer. People _____ stop using aerosol sprays.

5. Some companies continue to dump harmful chemicals in our lakes and rivers. Governments _____ pass strict laws against it.

6. Disposable products such as plastic razors waste natural resources. We _____ buy disposable products.

7. Burning garbage creates toxic gases that pollute the air we breathe. We _____ burn our garbage.

8. Glass can easily be recycled into new products. We _____ recycle glass jars and bottles.

9. The ozone layer lets dangerous rays pass through. We _____ expose our skin to direct sunlight.

10. The average Canadian household produces one tonne of garbage a year. We _____ cut back on waste in our society.

THE THREE Rs

 A   Read the three paragraphs and match one of the words below to each paragraph.

reduce   reuse   recycle

1. You can write on both sides of a piece of paper. When you buy food that comes in a plastic container, you can use the container later to keep other food fresh. You can give clothes that you do not wear any more to other people. You can use many things more than once.

2. If you change your buying habits, you will not have so much garbage in the first place. Try not to buy disposable items such as plastic razors or paper cups. Try to buy products that do not have a lot of packaging. Do not buy things that you do not really need.

3. Many items can be used again in a different way. For example, glass bottles can be melted and made into new bottles. Plastic from food containers can be made into park benches. Newspapers can be used to make cardboard and other paper products. Do not throw everything you don't need into the garbage.

  B   Close your book and work with a partner. See how many of the suggestions you can remember for each of the three Rs. Write them in your notebook.

DOING WHAT WE CAN

 LISTENING ACTIVITY 2

  A   Discuss these questions in a group.

1. What are some problems in the environment today?

2. What are people in your city or town doing to help the environment?

3. What do you do to help the environment?

  B   Read the questions aloud with a partner.

  C   Listen for the main ideas. Answer these three questions:

1. What kind of group is Tara involved in?

2. How do many young people feel about the environment?

3. Where can people get information about the environment?

  D   Listen again for details. Choose the topics you hear information about.

1. Which of the following environmental problems are mentioned?

   a) air pollution
   b) water pollution
   c) acid rain
   d) global warming
   e) too much garbage
   f) endangered species
   g) noise pollution
   h) deforestation

2. Which of these things do Tara and her friends do?

   a) join a community
      environmental group
   b) plant trees
   c) become vegetarian
   d) use natural products
   e) recycle glass and paper
   f) join an animal-rights group
   g) use cloth bags for shopping
   h) start an environmental
      newsletter
   i) plant vegetables
   j) join a "save the whales" group
   k) turn out the lights when they
      leave the room

  E   After you listen, discuss these questions in a group.

1. What are some common sense things people can do to help the environment?

2. Can you think of any new things you could do to help the environment?

JOURNAL

Write about some problems in our environment, and some solutions. What do you do personally to help the environment? What other things could you do?

PROBLEM SOLVING

What Would You Do?

You would like to do your share to help the environment. In a group, talk about some things you could do in these situations.

1. There is no paper recycling in your school or office. You notice that people throw away a lot of paper.

2. Your local supermarket seems to wrap everything in paper and styrofoam, including most of the vegetables and fruits. If you want to buy a single lemon or green pepper, it is usually wrapped in plastic.

3. You would like to plant some vegetables in your garden, but you are not sure which ones will grow well, or how to take care of them.

4. At the supermarket, some of the products you buy come in different kinds of containers. For example, you can get orange juice in a plastic carton or a glass bottle. The price is about the same for each. How do you decide which to buy?

5. The people at your office drink a lot of coffee, and most of them use a new styrofoam cup each time they have a drink. At the end of each day there is a garbage can filled with styrofoam cups.

How Green Are You?

Complete this puzzle with words from the unit. Use the worksheet.

 Across

4. Many things we buy are wrapped in layers of _____.

6. After you have finished with a glass jar you can put it in the blue box to _____ it.

7. Foods that are put on styrofoam trays usually have _____ wrap on top.

9. Aluminium cans are made of _____ that can be recycled.

10. Plastic is made from _____ that comes from the ground.

11. A lot of garbage is dumped into bodies of water such as rivers and _____.

15. During the manufacturing process, _____ are released into the air.

16. Every day _____ of trees are cut down to make paper and cardboard.

19. Recycling boxes are usually green or _____.

Down

1. When our garbage is collected, it is taken to a _____ site.
2. Trees are cut down to get newsprint and other kinds of _____.
3. We use _____ to make boxes and other kinds of food containers.
4. Dumping chemicals into rivers and oceans causes water _____.
5. After you have used a bottle, you can usually _____ it with other liquids.
8. One way to avoid excess packaging is to _____ the number of bags you use.
12. We use _____ to make coffee cups and other kinds of food containers.
13. If you use _____ bags, you will not need to get plastic or paper bags from stores.
14. To save plastic and paper, try not to use _____ items such as plastic razors and paper plates.
17. The largest use of aluminium is in cans for soft _____.
18. If you throw away a bottle made of _____ in a forest, it will last a very long time.

IN YOUR HOME

Read the information. Check your ideas from Exercise B on page 14.

Family A helps the environment in these ways:

1. Uses a phosphate-free detergent to protect our water system. Phosphates contribute to water pollution.
2. Bought a few inexpensive cloth bags to use when shopping for groceries. Now they don't take home a lot of paper or plastic bags.
3. Recycles bottles, jars, and cans in their blue recycling box.
4. Recycles newspapers, paper, and cardboard
5. Buys large size packages of food when possible, to reduce the amount of packaging and number of containers
6. Uses plastic lunch boxes and thermos flasks, with re-usable plastic food containers, rather than paper bags and plastic wrap that they throw away.
7. Uses a compost bin for food scraps, rather than throwing food scraps in the garbage.
8. Uses cloth dish towels and rags for cleaning, rather than paper towels.
9. Turns off the lights when they leave the room.
10. Uses ceramic mugs rather than styrofoam cups.
11. Uses real cutlery and dishes rather than paper and plastic products.
12. Uses natural household cleaners such as vinegar and baking soda whenever possible, instead of strong chemicals

Family B harms the environment in these ways:

1. Uses a detergent with phosphates that contributes to water pollution.
2. Uses paper or plastic bags when grocery shopping.
3. Throws bottles, jars, and cans into the garbage.
4. Throws newspapers, paper, and cardboard into the garbage.
5. Buys small containers of food that have a lot of packaging.
6. Uses plastic or paper lunch bags and plastic wrap for food.
7. Throws food scraps into the garbage.
8. Uses paper towels for cleaning.
9. Leaves the lights on when they leave the room.
10. Often uses styrofoam cups.
11. Often uses plastic cutlery and paper plates.
12. Uses strong chemical household cleaners.

THE GARBAGE QUIZ

C   Read the information. Check your answers to the quiz on pages 17-18.

1. About one third of all the garbage we throw out is made of paper. Another third comes from food scraps. The final third is a mixture of glass, metal, plastic, and wood.

2. Most of the garbage that is collected is dumped in a hole known as a landfill site.

3. Landfill sites are filling up quickly. In many cities, landfill sites are closing because there is no more room for garbage. City and provincial governments have to find new ways to deal with our garbage.

4. Burning garbage releases chemicals into the air. Many of these chemicals are harmful to our health.

5. Styrofoam, a kind of plastic, is used to make fast-food containers, take-out coffee cups, and many other things. Every day, thousands of tonnes of styrofoam are thrown out. If we used all the styrofoam that people in North America threw out in one day, we could make 900 million styrofoam coffee cups!

6. Every year North Americans throw away over 16 billion disposable diapers, one and a half billion plastic pens, over two billion plastic razors, and 220 million car tires.

7. If you throw a glass bottle away in a forest, it will last a long time. It will still be there for your great-grandchildren to see. In fact, it will last for about a thousand years.

8. Aluminium is used to make airplanes, cars, household items, and many other things. The largest use of aluminium is in cans for drinks such as soft drinks and beer.

9. It is much more expensive to make a new can from metal than to recycle a can. The energy saved from recycling one can would be enough to power your television set for three hours.

10. The number of trees that are cut down every day to make paper for Canada's newspapers is over 40 000. This is the total number of trees in many forests!

11. We use plastic for many things, from combs to pens to razors. Half of all the plastic we use, however, is in the form of packaging, including plastic bags from supermarkets and other stores.

12. When you spend $10 on food, about one dollar is spent on the packaging and bags you use to take the food home. This packaging is thrown away as soon as you get home.

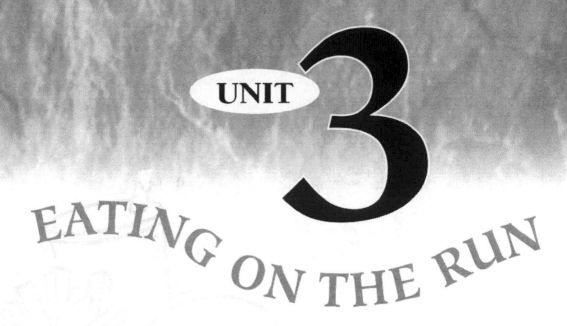

EATING ON THE RUN

WHAT'S THE FOOD?

A Work in a group. Match the foods on the list with the clues below.

**chocolate   a watermelon   milk   a pineapple   a cucumber
spaghetti   olives   ice cream   a banana   cheese**

1. a cold, sweet food that comes in many flavours

2. small green or black fruits used to make oil

3. a large fruit that is red inside with many seeds

4. a food made from flour that is eaten with sauce

5. a white beverage that is popular with children

6. a food made from milk that is good in sandwiches

7. a sweet treat that is used in cookies and cakes

8. a long yellow fruit that is white inside

9. a vegetable that is green outside and white inside

10. a sweet yellow fruit that grows in the tropics

29

B   Match the food to the country it comes from.

1.   shish kebab   a)   Mexico

2.   egg rolls   b)   France

3.   borscht   c)   Russia

4.   sushi   d)   Japan

5.   lasagna   e)   Canada

6.   satay   f)   China

7.   tacos   g)   Iran

8.   croissants   h)   Indonesia

9.   hamburgers   i)   Italy

10. maple syrup   j)   the United States

TALK ABOUT IT

Work in groups. First, tell your group what culture you come from. Then describe a popular food in your culture.

LET'S TAKE A BREAK

A Read this paragraph. Then close your book and write as the teacher dictates it.

> Whether people work at home, in factories, in offices, or in schools, there is probably one custom that they share. It's called the coffee break. The strange thing about a coffee break is that people don't necessarily drink coffee. They may drink tea or juice or simply eat an apple!

B Read the text and answer the questions **orally** with a partner.

Let's Take a Break

One of the most popular beverages in Canada is coffee. Fifty-seven percent of Canadians drink coffee every day. Of course, there are some people who don't drink coffee at all. They prefer tea or soft drinks, or even water. Coffee isn't a drink for children either. Many people avoid drinking coffee before bedtime. They are afraid it will keep them awake. The biggest consumers of coffee are people between the ages of 30 and 50. They drink an average of 3.75 cups of coffee a day!

Coffee is a traditional breakfast drink. Canadians like to eat eggs with toast or pancakes and have a cup of coffee before they start the day. Many people also like to have a cup of coffee after dinner in the evening. They may have a cup of espresso or a cup of coffee with milk or sugar with their dessert. Sixty-six percent of the coffee Canadians drink is consumed at home.

Coffee shops have become a fast-growing business. The coffee shop is a regular stop on the way to work for many people. A large part of coffee shop business is take-out orders. People stop in and order coffee to go. Everyone has a personal preference. The coffee can be served with cream, milk, one sugar, or two sugars.

At work, coffee breaks provide a pause in the day's routine. Once in the morning and once in the afternoon, everyone stops work and heads for the coffee room. In many workplaces, employees have coffee pools. This means they put their money together to rent a coffee machine and buy supplies such as coffee, milk, sugar, and cups. Other companies have coffee supplies delivered, as a way of keeping their employees happy.

Nevertheless, during coffee breaks, you often hear the comment, "Oh dear, I'll have to stop drinking so much coffee. It's making me nervous." In fact, some workplaces have started to replace the term "coffee break" with "health break." This is a coffee break without coffee. Workers may stop work and eat an apple instead of drinking a cup of coffee. Too much coffee can make people nervous and difficult to get along with. Still, coffee remains popular in Canada. Canadians consumed $1 billion dollars' worth of coffee in the last year alone!

1. What percentage of people in Canada drink coffee every day?

2. Who doesn't drink coffee?

3. Why do some people not want to drink coffee before bedtime?

4. Which group of Canadians drinks the most coffee?

5. Name some foods Canadians eat for breakfast.

6. What do people have with their coffee after dinner?

7. What does "coffee to go" mean?

8. What are some of the ways coffee is served?

9. When do people take coffee breaks at work?

10. Describe how a coffee pool works.

11. Why do some companies have coffee supplies delivered?

12. What is a "health break"?

13. Name one bad effect of coffee.

14. How much coffee did Canadians drink last year?

C Read the text again and write answers to the questions.

EATING OUT

 Work in pairs. Complete the paragraphs with the words below.

cities groups birthdays sections budget restaurants romantic tablecloths past relatives

Eating out in __1_____ is more popular in Canada now than it was in the __2_____. Today, meeting friends, __3_____, or colleagues at a restaurant is a common way of celebrating __4_____, holidays, or other special occasions. There are menus for every __5_____ too.

Chinese restaurants are popular with big __6_____. French restaurants are a good place for __7_____ dining, with linen __8_____ and good cutlery and china. In big __9_____, there are lots of other choices too, from Japanese to Indian to Turkish food. Restaurants today also offer a choice of smoking or non-smoking __10_____.

TALK ABOUT IT

A Work in a group to discuss these questions.

1. Name a food or foods that you don't like.

2. Are there any foods you really hate?

3. Why do you dislike or hate these foods?

4. Would you ever eat these foods? If so, in what circumstances?

5. Are there any foods that you don't eat for health or religious reasons?

B Do a survey. Walk around the classroom and ask people about foods they dislike. Write their names and the foods.

C In your groups, compare notes. See if you can find three foods that most people dislike.

WHERE SHOULD WE EAT?

LISTENING ACTIVITY 3

A Match the foods that the people listed would **not** want to eat.

1. a "meat-and-potatoes person"   a)   an ice-cream sundae

2. a vegetarian   b)   a large steak

3. a student on a budget   c)   tofu and brown rice

4. a gourmet chef   d)   a five-course dinner

5. a young child   e)   a garlic and onion pizza

6. a person on a diet   f)   a hot dog and fries

7. a couple on a date   g)   a plate of broccoli and peas

B   Read the questions aloud with a partner.

C   Listen and answer the questions.

1. When are Sophie and Mike free for dinner?

2. What kind of restaurant does Rosa suggest?

3. What two reasons does Sophie give for not wanting to go there?

4. What kind of restaurant does Sophie suggest?

5. What kind of food does Tom like to eat?

6. What kind of food does Sophie suggest next?

7. Why does Rosa not want to go there?

8. Why is Chinese food a good choice?

9. What two things does Sophie say about the food in the new Chinese restaurant?

10. What will Sophie do to make sure they get a table?

Turn to page 40 for Exercise D.

 **Past Continuous**

Use the past continuous to focus on an action **in progress** in the past. Use the past continuous for an action that was not finished when it **was interrupted**.

> I was cooking when the phone rang.

Use the past form of the auxiliary verb **be** (**was**, **were**) to show **past time**. Use the **ing** form of the main verb to show that the action was in progress.

A   Put the verbs in the past continuous form.

1. A radio _____ (play) in the background when I arrived.

2. Mary _____ (eat) dinner so she didn't answer the phone.

3. The neighbours _____ (make) a lot of noise last night.

4. When I saw Franco, he _____ (run) to catch the bus.

5. Someone else _____ (use) the tennis courts so we had to wait.

6. The people who sat near us _____ (celebrate) a birthday.

7. At 8:30 yesterday morning John _____ (finish) his second coffee.

8. The class _____ (have) a break when Jennifer got there.

9. When the guests arrived, the hostess _____ (set) the table.

10. Everyone _____ (carry) an umbrella this morning. They thought it was going to rain.

B   At 10 p.m. last night the fire alarm in the apartment building rang. Write sentences in your notebook about what the neighbours were doing.

Past Continuous: Negative

For the negative form of the past continuous, add **not** after the auxiliary verb **be**. The contraction is **wasn't** or **weren't**. Use the **ing** form of the main verb.

A Write the sentences in the negative form. Use the contraction.

1. Mike _____ (work) very hard yesterday.

2. My friends _____ (study) enough last term.

3. Lili _____ (feel) well when I saw her.

4. Kengo was tired so he _____ (do) his homework.

5. My cousins _____ (live) in residence last year.

6. Keiko _____ (eat) because she wasn't hungry.

7. It _____ (rain) so I didn't need my umbrella.

8. We felt impatient because the server _____ (bring) our food.

9. It was too hot because the air conditioner _____ (run).

10. They _____ (watch) TV. They were playing computer games.

Past Continuous: Questions

For the question form of the past continuous, put the auxiliary verb before the subject.

> **Was** she **waiting** for a phone call?

A Match the questions and the answers. Then write the answers as full sentences.

1. What were the players doing yesterday?

2. Why were the people running this morning?

3. When was the student sleeping?

4. Where was the exam taking place?

5. How were the new students feeling yesterday?

6. Who was preparing the food while the cook was away?

a) during the English class

b) practising for the game

c) the owner of the restaurant

d) a little bit nervous

e) to get out of the rain

f) in the auditorium

SNACK FOODS

A Work in a group to discuss these questions.

1. How often do you have a snack?

2. What kinds of snacks do you usually have?

3. How often do you eat something sweet as a snack or for dessert?

4. What kinds of snacks are healthy?

B Work in a group. Use the categories below to rate the snacks in the list. For example, which food is the most tasty? Which food is the least tasty? Write **1** for the most, and **10** for the least.

Try to reach a consensus in your group. Then compare your ratings with other groups.

Categories

a) tasty   b) healthy   c) expensive

Snacks

1. potato chips   7. a doughnut

2. a chocolate bar   8. ice cream

3. a granola bar   9. a bran muffin

4. cookies   10. a bagel

5. an apple   11. peanuts

6. carrot sticks   12. apple pie

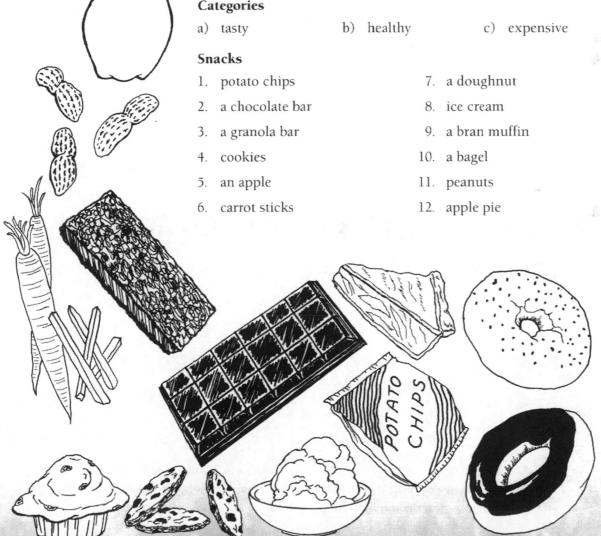

HAVING A SNACK

CBC

VIDEO ACTIVITY 2

A Read the questions aloud with a partner.

B Watch the video and answer the questions. Use the worksheet.

1. What do people traditionally have as a sweet snack?

2. Complete the chart.

	Calories	Grams of fat
A chocolate bar		
A granola bar		
A bagel		

3. Where do the calories in health bars come from?

4. Where does the fat come from?

5. How much Swiss chocolate was eaten last year?

6. Why is Swiss chocolate famous?

7. What has changed in the manufacturing of chocolate?

JOURNAL

Write about the kinds of foods you eat for meals and snacks.

CANADIAN CAPSULES

The first question you will likely be asked when you enter a restaurant is "Smoking or non?" This means, "Would you like to sit in the smoking section or in the non-smoking section?"

PROBLEM SOLVING

What Would You Say or Do?

A Work in pairs. Discuss what you would do and how you would say it in these situations. Then compare your suggestions with those of another pair.

1. Someone in the group suggests going out for hamburgers. You know that there are two vegetarians in the group.

2. You are in a restaurant with friends. When the bill comes, you realize that you don't have enough money to pay your share.

3. You have had more than enough to eat but your host or hostess is insisting that you eat some more.

4. You are still hungry after a meal at a friend's house but no one is offering you any more food.

5. When you get the bill in a restaurant, you notice that your dessert is not included on the bill.

6. You and your friends don't smoke. When you arrive at a restaurant, only tables in the smoking section are available. You are told that it will be a long wait for a table in the non-smoking section.

B Different cultures have different customs. What is normal in your culture?

1. Would you eat or drink before you were invited to do so by the hostess?

2. Would you say anything before starting to eat a meal?

3. How many times would something be offered before you accepted it?

4. What would you bring if you were invited for dinner?

5. At what time would it be normal to go home?
   a) right after dinner
   b) when the host and hostess go to bed
   c) when the hostess mentions that you must be tired
   d) when another guest leaves
   e) other (Explain.)

6. Would you offer to help clean up after dinner?

7. What would you do if you wanted to smoke a cigarette after dinner?

CANADIAN CAPSULES

An important custom in a sit-down restaurant is leaving a tip for the server. A tip is generally 10 to 15 percent of the cost of the meal before taxes. You should leave the tip on the table as you leave.

WHERE SHOULD WE EAT?

LISTENING ACTIVITY 3

D   Listen and complete the dialogue. Use the worksheet.

Rosa: Hi, Sophie. How _____ you and Mike?

Sophie: Pretty good, Rosa. How are you? How's Tom?

Rosa: We're fine. _____ you and Mike want to go out _____ eat with us this weekend?

Sophie: This weekend? Let's see. I think that should _____ all right. We have plans for Friday night, _____ Saturday night should be OK. What _____ you have in mind?

Rosa: Well, there's that good steak restaurant we went to a _____ months ago. What about that?

Sophie: I don't know. It _____ kind of expensive, and I don't really eat much meat anymore.

Rosa: Have _____ become vegetarian?

Sophie: Well, not completely. I still eat chicken _____ fish once in a while, but I don't eat _____ red meat. Would you like _____ try a new vegetarian restaurant I heard about?

Rosa: I don't know if Tom would go _____ that. He's a real meat-and-potatoes man. He's not really into this health food stuff. I don't think _____ go for a tofu and vegetable meal.

Sophie: I guess I understand. Mike's not too crazy about my choice _____ food either. What about Italian food?

Rosa: Well, I'm on _____ diet, and the food is pretty rich—all those sauces and cheeses.

Sophie: That's true. Well, _____ about Chinese food? There are lots of vegetable dishes, so you and I will both _____ happy. Mike and Tom can order some of the meat dishes they like.

Rosa: That's a good idea. _____ we order a few different things, we can each try _____ few dishes, and split the cost. I'm just dying for some _____ those delicious peanut butter dumplings.

Sophie: Me too. Let's go to _____ new Chinese restaurant on Park Street. The food is always fresh there, although some _____ the dishes are quite spicy.

Rosa: That's OK. We like spicy food. We'll meet _____ there at 8:00.

Sophie: Great. I'll call _____ make reservations so we'll be sure _____ get a table. It gets pretty busy there on the weekends.

Rosa: OK, see _____ there.

Sophie: 'Bye.

   E   Practise the conversation with a partner.

UNIT 4

SPORTS AND FITNESS

Look at the list of sports. Put the sports into the categories below. Some sports can go in more than one category. Add any other sports you can think of.

Categories

- sports you play on snow or ice
- sports you play on water
- sports you play indoors
- sports you can play outdoors
- sports you play in a team
- sports you play alone

Sports List

aikido	diving	judo	soccer
archery	fencing	karate	softball
badminton	field hockey	kayaking	swimming
boxing	football	luge	tobogganing
baseball	golf	rowing	volleyball
basketball	gymnastics	tennis	weightlifting
canoeing	hang gliding	sailing	wrestling
cricket	hockey	skating	
cycling	in-line skating	skiing	

SPORTS IN CANADA

 What do you know about sports? Work with a partner. Read the text on pages 43–45 quickly to find the answers to these questions.

1. What is Canada's national sport?

2. What are Canada's three most popular sports?

3. What is the "number one" sport in the world?

4. Which sport is called "the national pastime" in the United States?

5. Which sport began over 2500 years ago?

6. Which sport began in England?

7. Which sport is played in 150 countries in the world?

8. Which sport is generally used to improve one's looks?

9. Which sport was a completely new game about 100 years ago?

10. In which sport do teenage girls excel?

11. Which sports are played outdoors on frozen lakes and rivers?

12. Which sports were used only for self-defence in the past?

13. In which sport are grace, rhythm, and posture important?

14. Which sport is often done in resorts in the mountains?

15. For which sport did people once use animal bones and skins?

16. Which sport was invented by a Canadian?

17. Which sports were played every four years?

18. Which sport has a different name in some countries?

19. Which sport is extremely fast?

20. Which sport became known to the western world when it was accepted in the Olympics?

CANADIAN CAPSULES

The West Coast Trail in Pacific Rim National Park on Vancouver Island is so popular that Parks Canada had to set a limit on how many people can use the trail. People who want to hike there in summer must reserve in advance by calling a 1-800 number. It costs $25 to book a place.

Skiing

Millions of Canadians take part in one of this country's most popular sports: skiing. There are two main types of skiing. Alpine skiing consists of racing down the slopes of mountains. Nordic skiing includes cross-country skiing and ski jumping.

Every winter people head towards the mountains with their skis, boots, and poles. They stay at ski resorts in the mountains of Alberta, British Columbia, Ontario, and Quebec.

Gymnastics

Gymnastics takes a combination of strength, skill, and co-ordination. This sport began in ancient Greece, and is now a part of the Olympic Games. It consists of floor exercises and events on equipment such as bars, rings, and balance beams. It is a sport in which teenage girls often excel. Grace, rhythm, form, posture, and timing are all important in this sport.

Hockey

Hockey is Canada's national sport. During the winter, people across Canada attend hockey games in arenas, watch games on TV, and talk excitedly about the latest scores. In the past, all hockey games were played outside on frozen rivers and lakes, but today most hockey games take place in indoor arenas.

Hockey is a rough game that is played on ice. Two teams compete to score points by shooting a puck into a net. Each team has six players. Hockey is one of the fastest sports. When players shoot the puck, it can travel more than 160 kilometres per hour.

Ice Skating

Ice skating is a popular winter sport. Almost every community in Canada has an indoor rink, but many people still go skating on frozen ponds, lakes, and rivers. In fact, every winter the Rideau Canal in Ottawa is turned into the world's longest skating rink.

Ice skating began in Europe two thousand years ago. People used blades made of bone. In Canada, the Iroquois made skates out of animal bones and leather. Today, there are two kinds of competitive skating: figure skating, which is almost like ballet, and speed skating.

Baseball

Every year, millions of people in North America play this game with a bat and a ball. Millions more go to ball parks to watch major league teams compete. Even more people listen to games on the radio and watch them on television. Baseball is so popular in the United States that it is sometime called "the national pastime."

Baseball began in the United States in the 1800s, and gradually spread to other countries. Today, there are organized leagues for everyone, from young children to professionals.

Basketball

Basketball is a fast, exciting game. Opposing teams try to score points by shooting a ball into a basket at the end of a court. Basketball did not develop gradually, as many other sports did. It was a completely new game, invented in 1891 by a Canadian named James Naismith. At that time, Naismith was a teacher at a school in Springfield, Massachusetts. His goal was to create a game that could be played indoors, all year around. His first baskets were made of wood. The game quickly gained popularity, and by the mid-1900s had become the world's most popular indoor sport.

The Olympic Games

The Olympic Games began in Greece over 2500 years ago. When they began in 776 BC, there was only one event—the footrace. Later other events, such as wrestling, boxing, and the pentathlon, were added. For over 1000 years, the Olympic Games took place every four years, until AD 393, when they were stopped by a Roman Emperor. In 1875, a French educator, Pierre de Coubertin, organized the first modern Olympic Games.

Today the Olympic Games consist of separate events for the Summer and Winter Olympics. The summer games include basketball, judo, swimming, tennis, volleyball, and many other events. Winter games include different kinds of skiing, skating, and ice hockey.

Soccer

Soccer is the "number one" sport in the world. In most European and Latin-American countries it is the national sport. It is estimated that it is played by over one billion people in over 150 countries around the world. In Great Britain and many other countries, soccer is called "football."

The World Cup, soccer's most famous international competition, is held every four years. Teams from more than 100 countries participate, with the top 24 teams representing their nations in a three-week tournament.

Swimming

Swimming is an international sport. It is popular because it is fun and provides good exercise. People of all ages swim in indoor pools and in lakes, rivers, and oceans. Most communities and many schools, recreation centres, and apartment buildings have indoor or outdoor pools for local residents.

Swimming is one of the highlights of the Summer Olympics. Athletes compete in various events that range from 50 to 1500 metres.

Tennis

Millions of people play tennis for exercise and recreation. Tennis is played on courts in private clubs and in public parks, both indoors and outdoors. It is also one of the world's most popular spectator sports, with thousands of fans attending tournaments and millions more watching the matches on TV.

Tennis began in England in the late 1800s, and quickly spread to other countries. Today over 2 million people play tennis in Canada. It is the third most popular sport, after swimming and ice skating.

The Martial Arts

The term "martial" comes from Mars, the Roman god of war. The martial arts include judo, aikido, kung fu, and other sports that originate in China, Japan, and Korea. The martial arts were once used only for defence. In 1964, when judo was accepted as an Olympic sport, it became known in the western world. Today people all over the world practise the martial arts both for self-defence and for the confidence that comes with learning these skills.

Weightlifting

People lift weights for exercise and to develop their muscles. For some people, weightlifting is a competitive sport. They compete to see who can lift the heaviest weight. For other people, it is a hobby. Body-builders lift weights to improve their muscle tone, and to improve their general health. They develop their muscles by increasing the weights they lift. There are body-building competitions for both men and women, but most people lift weights just because they want to look good.

PHYSICAL FITNESS

 Work in pairs. Complete the paragraphs with the words below.

**energy   shape   injury   bending   muscles   lungs
exercise   fit   tired   cycling**

Being physically __1_____ allows you to perform well in physical activities without getting __2_____. People who are physically fit have lots of __3_____ and are in good health.

Regular exercise helps people increase the capacity of their hearts and __4_____. Most experts agree that 30 minutes of __5_____, three times a week, is the minimum needed to keep people in __6_____.

A workout should consist of three basic exercise types—flexibility, endurance, and strength. Flexibility exercises, such as __7_____ and turning, strengthen the tissues and joints and prevent __8_____. Endurance exercises, such as running and __9_____, strengthen the heart and lungs. Strength exercises build and tone __10_____.

GETTING IN SHAPE

LISTENING ACTIVITY 4

A Read the questions aloud with a partner.

B Listen and answer the questions.

1. When does Bob play hockey?

2. Why does Jun want to play a sport?

3. What does Jun mean when he says he's become a "couch potato"?

4. Why doesn't Jun want to try out for the hockey team?

5. What is Jun interested in doing?

6. Which two places does Bob recommend?

7. Which two benefits does the health club have?

8. What do people need if they want to use the sports facilities at colleges or universities?

9. What two things does Jun want to find out about at the Y and the health clubs?

Turn to page 53 for Exercise C.

Gerunds as Subjects and Objects

A gerund is made by adding **ing** to a verb, but it functions as a noun. A gerund can function as the subject or the object of a sentence. It can also function as the object of a preposition.

Subject: **Swimming** is good exercise.

Object: I like **riding** a bicycle.

Object of a preposition: He is interested in **jogging**.

A Work in pairs. Match the subjects to the gerunds.

1. **Rest** helps relax the body.	a)	smoking
2. **Aquatic exercise** is good for you.	b)	dancing
3. **Ballet** develops the leg muscles.	c)	telling jokes
4. **Cigarettes** are bad for the lungs.	d)	watching TV
5. **Baseball** is a social activity.	e)	swimming
6. **Humour** makes people laugh.	f)	running
7. **Television** can be an obsession.	g)	working out
8. **Aerobic exercise** is good for the heart.	h)	camping out
9. The **footrace** was a sport in ancient Greece.	i)	lying down
10. **A tent in the back yard** is popular with children.	j)	playing ball

B   Identify the gerunds in the following sentences.

1.   You can stay fit by exercising every day.

2.   Try jogging or tai chi if you want free exercise.

3.   Too much sitting around isn't good for you.

4.   People feel better after sleeping well all night.

5.   A sure way to damage your skin is sunbathing.

6.   Walking to work is a good way to get exercise.

7.   Everyone knows that smoking is bad for the health.

8.   Overeating makes people put on weight quickly.

9.   Eating fruits and vegetables is good for your body.

10.   Nobody is really fond of doing push-ups.

C   Find the prepositions. Then complete the sentences with the gerund form of the verbs below.

arrive   win   see   bring   ski   get   say   lose   practise   play

1.   My friends are excited about _____ the concert.

2.   The players are tired of _____ for the game.

3.   Is anyone here interested in _____ tennis?

4.   Some people are really good at _____ down mountains.

5.   The crowd applauded them for _____ the championship.

6.   Don't leave without _____ "thank you" to the hostess.

7.   Did anyone think about _____ the football?

8.   He irritated everyone by _____ at practise late.

9.   We were tired of _____ up early to work out.

10.   Aerobics is a good way of _____ weight quickly.

CANADIAN CAPSULES   Close to 200 000 Canadians are members of the Canadian Figure Skating Association. Seventy-five percent of members are children who take skating lessons.

A   Read the story. Then, with a partner, answer the questions that follow **orally**.

The Art of Defence

Stuart Cowan

In today's violent society you should know how to defend yourself in case of physical attack. "It's just a good idea to know some form of self-defence," says Simon Raybould, a first-degree black belt and karate instructor at a YMCA. "Karate brings about a certain amount of confidence, whether you're a man, woman, or child."

Confidence is exactly what Jimmy Pascual was looking for when he started taking karate courses at the YMCA. "After university I had gained a lot of weight. So I figured karate would be a good way to get in shape and learn how to defend myself at the same time. It's also a good way to work out the stress from your job. I just feel more confident now."

Raybould, 20, has been teaching for two years after taking up karate at an early age. "I've always been interested in martial arts," he said. "It's a good form of physical fitness, but there are a million reasons why people take up karate."

When people think of martial arts, karate and judo usually come to mind. "The difference between karate and judo could be compared to the difference between wrestling and boxing," Raybould says. "Judo is more grappling, grabbing someone and throwing them to the ground, while karate is striking—kicking and punching."

The ultimate reward in martial arts is a black belt, and it takes an average of 5½ years of karate courses to gain a black belt.

"The number of belts before black varies but at the YMCA we have six belts before black—white, yellow, orange, green, blue, and brown," Raybould said. Originally there were just white and black belts, but people—especially in North America and Europe—want to feel progression, so the lower belts were introduced as stepping stones toward the black.

In today's society, karate holds important benefits for women in particular. "I strongly recommend that women learn some form of self-defence" says Catherine Bernard, who operates a karate school. "I was growing very concerned about the increasing violence in society and that's why I enrolled in a self-defence course in the first place. I have a lot of confidence now. A few women in my class have had to use karate and they've been 100 percent successful…it's a surprise thing. An attacker usually doesn't expect a woman to fight back."

Reprinted by permission of *The Gazette* (Montreal).

1. Why does Simon Raybould say it's a good idea to know self-defence?

2. What was Jimmy Pascual looking for when he started taking karate courses?

3. In what three ways did he think karate would help him?

4. How long has Raybould been teaching karate?

5. What is the difference between karate and judo?

6. What is the most important award in the martial arts?

7. How long does it generally take to get a black belt?

8. What are the colours of the belts given at the YMCA?

9. Why were the lower belts introduced in North America and Europe?

10. Why does Bernard recommend that women learn self-defence?

11. Why have women been successful when using karate?

B Answer the questions in writing. Use your notebook.

SPORTS PRESENTATION

Prepare a five-minute presentation about a sport you know. Give information about the following points:

Part A

What is the sport?

Do you play it yourself?

How long have you played it?

Where do you play it?

How often do you play it?

What season do you play it in?

How long did it take you to learn it?

Part B

What are the rules?

What special clothing or equipment is needed to play?

Are any special skills needed?

Part C

What risks are involved?

What benefits do you get from playing this sport?

To whom would you recommend this sport?

JOURNAL

Write about a sport that you play or that you like to watch. Use the information in the previous activity to help you.

PROBLEM SOLVING

How Much Does it Cost?

How much does it cost to do each of these? Discuss in groups.

1. buy a one-day ski-pass for Whistler Mountain in British Columbia
2. buy a bathing suit
3. join a health club for one year
4. join the YMCA or YWCA for one year
5. buy a bicycle
6. buy in-line skates
7. go to a play-off hockey game
8. rent a small sailboat for a day
9. take a walk in a park

10. buy a tennis racket
11. take an aerobic-exercise class
12. buy weight-training machines for your home
13. buy a can of tennis balls
14. buy a pair of running shoes
15. go to a baseball game
16. play 18 holes of golf at a public course
17. swim in a community pool
18. buy cross-country ski equipment

19. buy figure skates
20. see a Toronto Blue Jays home game at the SkyDome
21. buy a bicycle helmet
22. take a tennis lesson
23. buy a hockey stick
24. buy a snowboard
25. buy a set of golf clubs

The Sports Puzzle

Use these clues to complete the puzzle. Use the worksheet.

Across

2. You can swim in a lake or in a _____.

4. The sport that is called the "national pastime" in the United States is _____.

6. The most popular sport in the world is _____.

9. Karate and judo are often practised for self-_____.

12. Some sports are played alone. Others are played in a _____.

13. In winter, many people like to _____ indoors, in an arena, or outdoors, on a frozen lake or pond.

15. _____ is generally played indoors. It was invented by a Canadian.

16. Every summer people go _____ outdoors. When the weather is cold, they practise this sport indoors.

17. Hockey is played on _____ in an arena.

19. If you want to ski, you will have to go to the _____.

Down

1. Canada's national sport is _____.

3. Karate and _____ are two kinds of martial arts.

5. People skate outdoors or indoors in _____.

6. People play sports to increase their _____, flexibility, and endurance.

7. People do _____ to increase their strength and the size of their muscles.

8. Teenage girls often excel in _____.

10. Judo and _____ are both martial arts.

11. This popular sport is played on a court, with rackets and a ball.

14. The highest level belt in karate is a _____ belt.

18. In ancient Greece, the Olympic Games took place every _____ years.

GETTING IN SHAPE

LISTENING ACTIVITY 4

C Match the explanations below to the expressions in bold on page 54.

1. not in condition

2. an obsessive TV watcher

3. their prices

4. the most modern

5. practice time

6. try for a place on the team

Bob: Hi Jun. How's it going?

Jun: Not bad, Bob. How about you?

Bob: Pretty good. We had a great game this afternoon. Our team won!

Jun: Do you mean hockey?

Bob: Yeah, I play in a league in my neighbourhood. We get **ice time** at the arena every Tuesday afternoon. How about you? What do you play?

Jun: Well, actually not much lately. Since I moved here, I haven't been doing any sports. I want to do something because I'm really getting **out of shape**.

Bob: Do you like team sports?

Jun: Not that much. I mean, I like to watch them on TV, but I'm not really into playing on a team. I guess I've become a bit of a **couch potato**.

Bob: I know what you mean. It's easy to sit back and eat junk food and watch TV. Hey, maybe you could **try out** for our team.

Jun: I don't think so—I'm not really a good skater. I was thinking about doing some weightlifting—you know, body-building, but I'm not sure where.

Bob: Oh, that's easy—you can go to the Y, or you can join a health club. The health clubs might be a little more expensive, but they usually have **the latest** equipment, and they have a trainer to get you started.

Jun: That's an idea. What about at the universities and colleges? I heard they sometimes have sports facilities.

Bob: That's true. A lot of schools have sports facilities. If you have a student card, it doesn't cost much to join, and you can take classes, play on a team, swim....

Jun: Well, you've given me a few places to start. I think I'll call the college in my area. I wouldn't mind swimming a couple of times a week. I'm also going to call the Y and a few health clubs to find out **their rates** and schedules.

Bob: Let me know what you find out. I might want to do a little body-building myself.

   D   Practise the dialogue with a partner.

5
ALL YEAR ROUND

THE SEASONS

Work in a group. Discuss these questions.

1. Which countries have four seasons?

2. Which countries have two seasons?

3. Describe the four seasons in Canada.

4. What are some signs of the seasons changing?

5. What are some activities associated with each season?

6. Can you think of any difficulties people have to cope with in any of the seasons?

7. What is your favourite season? Why?

WINTER, SPRING, SUMMER, AND FALL

In which season is each of these most likely in Canada? Work in pairs to discuss the statements and write the season. (Some things can happen in more than one season).

1. Birds fly south.

2. Snow ploughs push snow to the sides of the street.

3. People rake leaves in their gardens.

4.   People go to the country to pick apples.

5.   People sit outside on their balconies in the evening.

6.   The city puts up no-parking signs.

7.   Ontario peaches are ripe.

8.   Snow melts and rivers overflow.

9.   Quebec maple syrup is ready.

10.   People change the tires on their cars.

11.   People plant flowers in their gardens.

12.   Local strawberries are ripe and ready to pick.

13.   Many baby animals are born on farms.

14.   People clean their houses from top to bottom.

15.   City workers scatter salt on the roads.

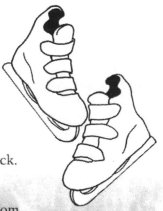

16. Birds wake you up at 5:00 a.m.

17. Fruits and vegetables are harvested.

18. People sit outdoors in restaurants and cafes.

19. Homes are heated.

20. People wear extra layers of clothes.

21. The sun sets around 4:30 p.m.

22. There are sudden thunderstorms, sometimes with hail.

23. It's cool in the morning and evening, but warm in the afternoon.

24. There's a chance of blizzards.

25. Daffodils bloom in British Columbia.

CHANGES

Read the paragraph. Then close your book and write while the teacher dictates.

The seasons are an important part of people's lives in Canada. Many parts of Canada have a wide range of temperatures, from very cold winters to warm or hot summers. People change their activities at different times of the year. They also make adjustments in their clothing and in their homes to cope with the different weather conditions. Houses in Canada are constructed with materials that can withstand temperature extremes, particularly the cold.

CANADIAN CAPSULES

Would you expect to see flowers budding in January in the snowy Canadian Prairies? Sometimes they do, when a warm dry wind blows across Alberta or Saskatchewan. This wind, called a Chinook, can raise the temperature more than 20° Celsius in one hour, and change winter into spring-like conditions. Animals come out of hibernation and flowers start to bloom.

WHAT IS IT?

Work in pairs. Match the words to the pictures.

1.   a snow shovel
2.   a bird feeder
3.   a scraper
4.   a snow plough
5.   a no-parking sign
6.   sand/salt
7.   snow tires
8.   a furnace
9.   a revolving door
10. a garden hose

11. a sprinkler
12. a pile of leaves
13. snow on a roof
14. a rake
15. a brick
16. a snow tractor
17. a patio
18. a barbecue
19. a fan
20. a vestibule

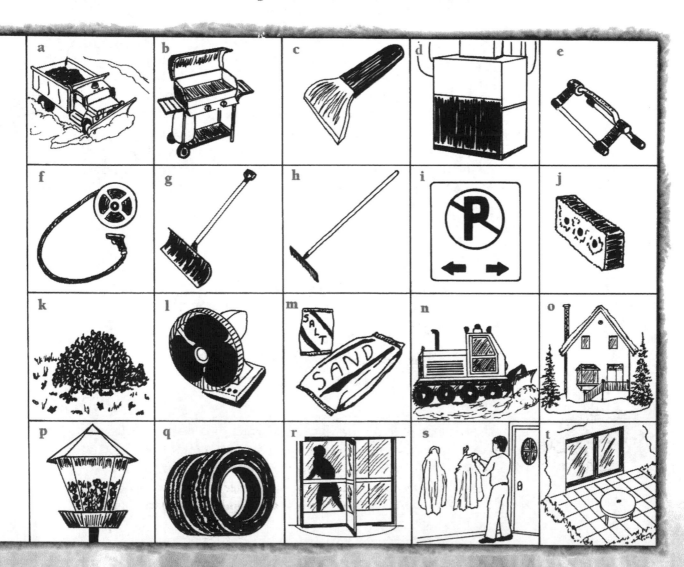

STORY EXCHANGE

A   Get ready.

1.   With a partner, choose one of the stories that follow (on page 59 or page 60).

2.   Read the story and answer the questions together **orally**.

Hibernation

In many parts of Canada, winter can begin as early as November and can continue well into March. People listen to the weather report often as they prepare for the first snowfall. They adjust their lifestyles to suit the weather. During the cold winter months, many people "hibernate." They close their doors, draw their curtains, and snuggle in their warm homes. For entertainment, they often invite friends to their homes.

Houses in countries with cold climates have several features that help keep them warm. Often the entrance to the house has a vestibule, which is a small room or area where people remove their boots in winter. The vestibule is often separated from the rest of the house by a door, which helps keep cold winds out of the house.

Inside the house, carpets keep heat from escaping through the floors, and curtains or drapes keep wind from coming in around the windows. Furniture and decorative items add a feeling of warmth as well.

Canadian houses are designed to retain heat. Many have insulation in the walls, and double windows and doors that keep the heat in and the cold out. The foundation is one of the most important parts of a building. It supports the house, and is built under the ground to keep the building stable when the earth freezes and thaws. Inside the foundation is the basement, a heated space that can be used in all seasons. It can be divided into several rooms, such as a family room, a storage room, and a utility room. Usually the furnace that heats the house is in the basement.

Houses in Canada are often made from brick, stone, and cement. These materials last a long time and provide excellent shelter from extreme cold. Homes are heated with different kinds of fuels. Oil and electric heating (often called hydro) are the most common, but natural gas is becoming more popular. Almost all homes have central heating, and most houses have a thermostat which makes it easy to adjust the temperature inside the house.

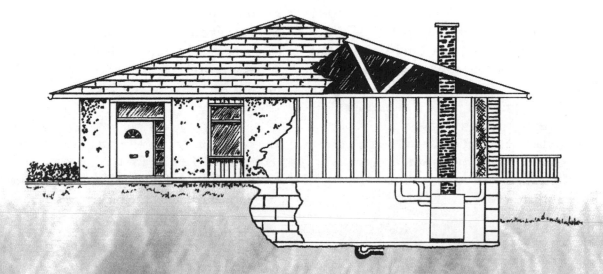

Questions

1. When does winter begin and end?

2. What do we mean when we say that people "hibernate" in their homes?

3. What is the purpose of a vestibule?

4. What are some of the items inside a house that keep heat from escaping?

5. How are houses in Canada designed to retain heat?

6. What is the purpose of the foundation?

7. What is a basement?

8. Where is the furnace?

9. Why are houses in Canada often made of brick, stone, or cement?

10. What are some common fuels used to heat homes?

11. What is a thermostat used for?

Outdoor Living

In spring, people who have hibernated in their homes all winter come outside. As the snow melts and the first flowers appear, people begin to take walks outside and enjoy meeting neighbours they haven't chatted with for several months.

After a long winter of being inside, many people clean their homes from top to bottom. Spring cleaning is a ritual for them, as they clean off the sand and salt that comes into their homes on their boots and clothing during the winter. People clean out their garages and hold garage sales to get rid of items they no longer need. Winter tires come off the cars, and people start planting flowers and trees.

In early spring, there can be a lot of rain, which may be followed by biting insects and blackflies in wooded areas. Spring can begin as early as March, but new leaves don't appear on trees until late April or May in most parts of Canada. The exception is southwestern British Columbia, which has a short, mild winter.

Summer can be very hot and humid in many parts of Canada. In fact, summer in parts of southern Canada can be as hot as any tropical country. To keep cool, people use fans or air conditioners.

Office buildings, stores, shopping centres, and movie theatres are air conditioned, and people can go indoors to cool off during the hottest part of the day.

Summer is such a short part of the year in Canada that people try to enjoy it as much as they can. It is a popular time for vacations, as people head to the beach or the mountains for summer sports and relaxation.

At home, people spend time on their balconies or patios, where families eat or barbecue food. Doors and windows are open, and people meet outside their houses. The streets in front of houses come alive with people walking, doing sports, watering their lawns, and gardening.

Early autumn is a beautiful time of year. The leaves change colours and the air turns cool. People shop for fresh vegetables at the public markets and drive to the country to see the glorious colours or to pick apples.

Questions

1.   What are some things people do when the snow melts?

2.   Why is spring cleaning a ritual?

3.   What are some things people don't like about early spring?

4.   When do leaves appear on trees in most parts of Canada?

5.   How hot can it get in summer in southern Canada?

6.   How do people keep cool in hot weather?

7.   Where do people go on summer vacations?

8.   Where do people sometimes eat in summer?

9.   What are some activities people do outside their homes in summer?

10.   What are some things people like to do in autumn?

B   Exchange stories.

Find a partner who read the other story. Close your books and use your own words to exchange information.

CANADIAN CAPSULES

In Canada, people live in big cities, small towns, suburban areas, and the country. Different styles of houses are built to accommodate different needs. The construction and materials of a house reflect the needs of the residents and the climate of the area. The materials used in construction are important factors in maintaining a comfortable temperature.

C   Review vocabulary.

Work with your partner. Match the items on the left with the functions or definitions on the right.

1. a basement   a) heats the house

2. a thermostat   b) cool the house

3. fans   c) supports the house

4. the foundation   d) regulates the temperature

5. a patio   e) where people remove their boots

6. a vestibule   f) where the family can eat

7. a garage   g) where the car is parked

8. carpets and curtains h) keep heating from escaping

9. a furnace   i) a heated space underground

GRAMMAR FOCUS — Present Simple versus Present Continuous

Use the present simple to refer to habitual actions or things in nature that do not change.

> I usually **take** the bus to work.
>
> It usually **snows** here in the winter.

Use the present continuous to focus on the moment that something is happening.

> It **is snowing** right now.

Use the present continuous for temporary situations.

> They **are travelling** in the Rockies.

A   Choose the present simple or the present continuous form of the verb.

1. It _____ (snow) a lot in Montreal in the winter.

2. The neighbours _____ (shovel) the snow in their driveway now.

3. Spring _____ (come) in the second quarter of the year here.

4. People in Canada _____ (enjoy) summer while they can.

5. Everyone _____ (swim) at the beach this afternoon.

6. Our neighbours _____ (cut) the grass every weekend.

7. Our neighbours _____ (cut) the grass right now.

8. Nobody _____ (stay) home today because it is sunny.

9. The leaves _____ (fall) from the trees in autumn.

10. Snow ploughs _____ (clear) the streets as fast as they can.

11. We _____ (want) to go swimming at the lake this weekend.

12. We know we are in Vancouver because it _____ (rain).

13. The man at the bus stop _____ (hold) an umbrella.

14. People here _____ (change) their activities each season.

15. Everyone _____ (look) out the window to see the snow.

B Change these sentences to the negative form. Choose **do** or **be** as the auxiliary verb.

1. Margo comes to class late.

2. Paula is speaking to the teacher.

3. Francisco speaks French well.

4. Barbara is visiting friends in Ottawa.

5. Po-Ling eats in the cafeteria.

6. Jean-Paul arrives at work first every day.

7. Lili comes from Hong Kong.

8. Hiroshi is studying English in Vancouver.

9. They are eating in my favourite restaurant.

10. It is raining outside at the moment.

11. Montreal has snowier winters than Toronto.

12. Juan likes to play tennis when it is raining.

13. It rains more in Victoria than in Vancouver.

14. The wind is blowing from the north today.

15. Moon-Hee is learning to play the violin this year.

CANADIAN CAPSULES

Because there is a lot of snow in many parts of Canada, houses often have steep roofs. The slopes stop the snow from staying on the roof and getting too heavy. The steep roof makes an attic inside the house, which can be used to store old clothes, furniture, and family souvenirs.

PLANNING A VACATION

LISTENING ACTIVITY 5

Canada has many great places to take vacations, from mountains to beaches to big cities.

A Work in a group. First, talk about which of these things you would like to do on a vacation. Then discuss where in Canada you could do them and at what time of year it would be best to do them.

1. see a waterfall
2. lie on the beach
3. go to a sugaring-off party
4. pick blueberries
5. hike in the mountains
6. go to a jazz festival
7. go snowshoeing
8. go to a ballet
9. eat in an outdoor cafe
10. visit an art museum

11. shop for souvenirs
12. go to the theatre
13. swim in the ocean
14. skate outdoors
15. ski in the mountains
16. go to the Caribana Festival
17. go on a ferry
18. go whale-watching
19. go ice fishing
20. camp out

B Read the questions aloud with a partner.

C Listen and answer the questions.

1. When do Peter and Ann plan to take their holidays?
2. What are they thinking of doing?
3. How does Peter plan on going to Vancouver Island?
4. What would Ann rather do?
5. When did the travel agent say they had to make up their minds?
6. Where did Ben go last summer?
7. What was the problem there?
8. Where does Ben plan to spend his holidays this year?
9. What three festivals does he plan to attend in Montreal?
10. How will he get to Toronto?
11. What two things does he mention about the Caribana Festival?
12. What does Ben like about outdoor festivals?

Turn to page 68 for Exercise D.

FOCUS ON PRONUNCIATION

When some words change from singular to plural, the vowel sound changes from short to long. Listen to your teacher say the words. Then practise with a partner.

1. a house   some houses
2. a roof   some roofs
3. a life   some lives
4. a thief   some thieves
5. a blouse   some blouses
6. a knife   some knives
7. a path   some paths
8. a leaf   some leaves
9. yourself   yourselves
10. a wife   some wives

SPRING EXCUSES

A   Answer these questions for yourself.

1. I take a day off school or work:
    a) never
    b) once in a while
    c) quite often

2. I would take a day off:
    a) if I was sick
    b) if I felt tired
    c) if someone in my family was sick
    d) for a medical appointment
    e) to do something enjoyable

3. If I take a day off:
    a) I always give the real reason
    b) I sometimes make up an excuse.

 B   Discuss your answers in a group. How many people gave the same answers?

C   Make a list of excuses you or people in your group have used. Then compare your list with the lists from other groups.

D   Read the questions aloud with a partner.

E   Watch the video and answer the questions. Use the worksheet.

1. When do Canadians need a few days to "goof off"?

2. How many days do Canadian workers take off every year?

3. Which six excuses about pets do people give for missing work?

a) My dog bit me.	f) My pet bird is ill.
b) My dog died.	g) My friend's mouse bit me.
c) I was bitten by a cat.	h) The family cat died.
d) I was bitten by a rabbit.	i) My parrot died.
e) My dog's sick.	j) My budgie died.

4. Which four excuses about cars do people give for missing work?

a) My car wouldn't start.

b) My car broke down.

c) The windshield wipers didn't work.

d) The brakes didn't work.

e) I couldn't get out of my driveway.

f) My car was towed away.

g) I lost my keys in a snowbank.

h) I misplaced my keys.

5. Which five general excuses do people give for missing work?

a) It was my mother's birthday.	f) I hadn't done my laundry.
b) It was my father's birthday.	g) I ate something and felt sick.
c) I had a headache.	h) My toilet overflowed.
d) I had a toothache.	i) My sink was blocked.
e) I had an earache.	j) My child was sick.

F   Talk about the video in your group. Which excuses did you think were the funniest? Did any of the excuses match yours? Which ones?

JOURNAL

Write about a vacation that you took, or a vacation you would like to take.

PROBLEM SOLVING

What Would You Do?

Discuss the situations below in a group.

1. You are asked to plan an outing for your class. Think of an interesting activity for the season you are in now, and for one other season. Explain what you would like to do and why.

2. You have just moved into your neighbourhood and would like to meet some people in your community. Think of some ways you could meet people at different times of the year.

3. You have a friend who is new to Canada and has never experienced winter. Make a list of things your friend needs to buy or do to prepare for his or her first winter.

What Do You Know?

Discuss these questions and answer **T** (true) or **F** (false).

1. There are penguins in the Canadian Arctic.

2. Golf and sailing are winter sports in Canada.

3. All the following creatures hibernate in winter: snakes, bears, frogs, squirrels.

4. In winter, people change the type of tires they use on their cars.

5. Cars use anti-freeze all year round.

6. Farmers harvest strawberries in the spring.

7. Pineapples grow in some parts of Canada.

8. Many houses have double windows as protection from winter cold.

9. Farmers harvest apples in the winter.

10. In Canada, you can ski in the month of April.

PLANNING A VACATION

LISTENING ACTIVITY 5

D   Listen and complete the dialogue.

Ben: Hi Peter. I heard you and Ann were going away for your holidays this summer.

Peter: You heard _____, Ben. We plan to go away for three weeks in July.

Ben: That's great. Where _____ you planning to go? Have you decided yet?

Peter: We aren't quite _____. We were thinking of taking a bicycle trip in B.C.

Ben: You mean biking in the area _____ Vancouver?

Peter: Not exactly. I love _____ ocean. I thought we'd take the ferry over to Vancouver Island and ride _____ bikes out to Long Beach.

Ben: Does Ann like biking?

Peter: Well, sort _____. We've agreed on B.C., but she would rather do some camping in the mountains.

Ben: Maybe you should flip _____ coin.

Peter: We may do _____. The travel agent said we had to make _____ our minds by next week. How about you, Ben? Any plans?

Ben: Well, last summer I went to P.E.I. The beaches were fantastic. The only problem _____ that I went in July and there were a _____ of people there. It was really hard to find space in the campgrounds.

Peter: Yes, I remember that you sent _____ a postcard with a picture of the beach. It looked beautiful. Do you think _____ go back this year?

Ben: No. I'm sticking closer to home. _____ a lot to do in Montreal in the summer. There's the Jazz Festival for one thing. A lot of _____ open-air performances are free.

Peter: What _____ is there to do?

Ben: There's the Film Festival _____ is really interesting and exciting. And "Just for Laughs."

Peter: What's that?

Ben: _____ a comedy festival. They have comedians from a
        lot of different countries. There are performances _____
        French and English. I might take the train down to Toronto
        _____.

Peter: What will you do in Toronto?

Ben: I'd like to take _____ the Caribana Festival. It's supposed
        to be really great, with music and fabulous costumes. I really like
        outdoor festivals. You know, the crowds, the excitement, and all
        that.

Peter: That sounds _____ a fun summer, Ben.

Ben: I hope _____. Well, nice talking to you.

Peter: You too! 'Bye.

   E   Practise the conversation with a partner.

IF YOU GET HURT

HEALTH CARE

Discuss these questions in a group.

1. Have you or someone you know had experience with the health-care system in this city?

2. What are some differences between health care here and in other places?

3. Do you know what the different steps are if you go to a hospital emergency room?

4. When would you call 911?

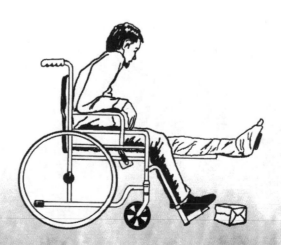

THE HUMAN BODY

 Look at the list of body parts below. Which ones are located:

a) above the neck

b) between the neck and the hips

c) below the hips

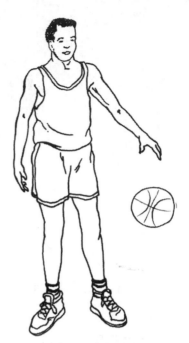

cheeks	esophagus
heart	knees
ankle	thumbs
stomach	wrists
liver	brain
trachea	heel
eyebrow	forehead
waist	thighs
toes	calves
jaw	arch
lungs	

THE BODY'S SYSTEMS

A   Read this paragraph. Then close your book and write the paragraph as the teacher dictates.

> Engineers have designed many wonderful machines, but no machine in the world comes close to the most incredible one of all: the human body. Our bodies are made up of many complex systems. These systems help our bodies grow, repair themselves, heal wounds, and fight infection. All of these systems work together to keep us healthy and strong.

CANADIAN CAPSULES   If you move from one province to another, you must re-register for your health insurance card.

B   Look at the picture. Use the labels in the diagram to complete the paragraphs about the body systems.

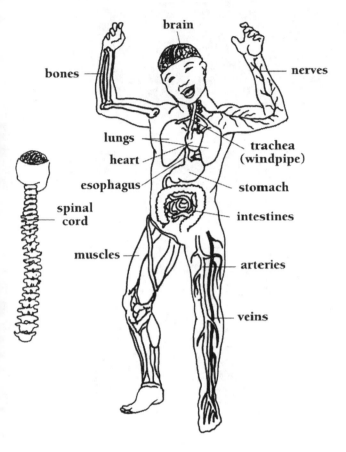

The Circulatory System

Every minute that you live, your __1_____ beats about 70 times. It pumps blood through the __2_____. The blood carries oxygen and food all over the body, and returns to the heart through the __3_____.

The Respiratory System

The __4_____ are in the chest. They help us breathe by taking in oxygen and releasing carbon dioxide. The air comes in through the nose and mouth, and then goes into the __5_____ to get into the body.

The Muscular and Skeletal Systems

To stand, walk, or do any physical activity, we need __6_____. They move the __7_____ that are part of the skeletal system. The skeleton keeps the body upright and protects internal organs.

The Digestive System

In order to function, the body needs fuel. We get this fuel through the food we eat. When we swallow, the food goes through the __8_____ and into the __9_____. Then the digestive system moves the food through the __10_____ where it is broken down into nutrients and absorbed into the bloodstream.

The Nervous System

Our five senses tell us about the world. Messages from our senses speed along a network of __11_____ to the __12_____, which has 14 billion nerve cells ready to process information and act on it. The __13_____, which runs along the backbone, also has many nerves that carry signals back and forth between the brain and the rest of the body.

Discuss these questions in a group.

1. What are some common kinds of accidents or injuries?
2. Which of these injuries are most serious?
3. What should you do to help someone who is injured?

ACCIDENTS AND INJURIES

A   Look at the pictures. Match the pictures to the words.

1. a burn
2. a cut
3. a broken bone
4. a sprained ankle
5. a heart attack
6. to choke
7. to be poisoned
8. frostbite
9. to faint
10. an upset stomach
11. a blister
12. to bleed
13. swollen
14. a bruise
15. a bump

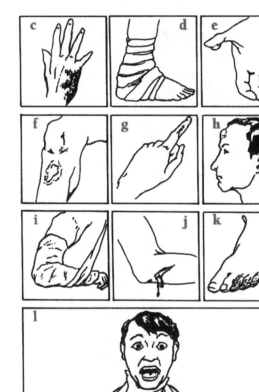

B Do you know what to do in an emergency? Do this quiz to find out. Work in a group. Choose the best answers.

1. To treat a burn:
   a) apply butter or a greasy substance
   b) immerse burned area in cool water
   c) immerse burned area in warm water

2. If someone starts to choke, you should:
   a) slap him or her on the back
   b) encourage him or her to talk
   c) encourage him or her to cough

3. The symptoms of frostbite are:
   a) skin irritation
   b) a white patch of skin
   c) a red patch of skin

4. Which of these could not be symptoms of a heart attack?
   a) pain in chest, neck, or shoulders
   b) weakness, nausea, shortness of breath
   c) coughing, sneezing, high fever

5. If someone is poisoned, you should give him or her:
   a) medication
   b) food
   c) water

6. The treatment for frostbite is:
   a) warm the area with a warm hand
   b) rub the area vigorously
   c) apply heat to the area

7. Someone's airway is completely obstructed if the person:
   a) is unable to speak or breathe
   b) cannot move
   c) is red in the face

8. If a person's clothing catches on fire:
   a) roll the victim in a coat or blanket
   b) use a fire extinguisher
   c) tell the victim to run

9. The Heimlich manoeuvre is:
   a) a new dance for teenagers
   b) a treatment for choking
   c) a method to help someone sober up

10. The parts of the body most susceptible to frostbite are:
    a) the legs
    b) the nose and cheeks
    c) the top of the head

CANADIAN CAPSULES Most dental services are not covered by provincial health plans, but many companies have dental plans as part of their employee benefit packages.

C Read the information from the Red Cross Safety card to check your answers.

BURNS

Tissue injuries resulting from over-exposure to excessive heat. Possible sources of heat include: thermal, chemical, electrical or radiation source (sun).

Types of burns

1st degree burn: Redness. This is a very minor burn, but can be very painful.

2nd degree burn: Redness and formation of blisters.

3rd degree burn: Charred-blackened appearance.

First Aid for burns

1st degree: Immerse the burned area in cool water at once.

2nd degree: Immerse the burned area in cool water at once. Do not break blisters.

3rd degree: Cover the entire burn lightly with a lint-free cloth.

Seek medical attention immediately.

Important notice

• Do not apply butter or other greasy substance to a burn.

• For eye burns caused by chemical splash, flush the eye(s) with large amounts of water for at least 10 minutes, including under eye lids from the inside to the outside. Ensure the drainage from the burned eye does not run into the other eye.

• If clothing catches on fire:
– restrain the victim from running;
– do not use a fire extinguisher;
– lie the victim on the ground;
– ask the victim to cover his/her face with the hands; and
– roll the victim in a blanket or large coat to smother the fire.

LIFE IS OUR CONCERN.

POISONING

When to suspect it:

• Any victim found unconscious, confused, or suddenly ill with suspected access to poisonous substance (usually children).

• Odor of poison on breath.

• Visible burns around the mouth.

• Open medicine or chemicals found in the presence of the victim.

• Sudden burning or pain in the throat.

Do...

1.   Immediately obtain medical assistance: hospital emergency room, Poison Centre, doctor, or family physician.

2.   Poison Centre phone number: (___) _____.

3.   If no medical assistance is available and if the victim is conscious, dilute poison by administering a non-toxic liquid (preferably water).

4.   Keep airway open.

5.   If victim vomits, turn victim on his or her side and retain sample.

6.   Start rescue breathing and/or cardiopulmonary resuscitation if necessary.

7.   Bring container of poison to hospital and have it on hand when calling the Poison Centre.

Do not...

1.   Give fluids to unconscious victim.

2.   Give ipecac or any other medication unless instructed to do so by medical personnel.

RED CROSS IS CONCERNED WITH YOUR SAFETY.

HEART ATTACK

When to suspect it:

Any victim who develops pain in the chest that may radiate to arms, shoulders, neck or jaw. Victim usually gets very weak, nauseated, and short of breath. Victim may perspire.

Do...

1.   Seek medical assistance immediately, preferably without leaving the victim.
2.   Place casualty in a comfortable position.
3.   Assist the casualty in taking medication if a prescription is at hand.
4.   Constantly check for victim's breathing and pulse.
5.   Ensure the casualty has a clear airway.
6.   Start rescue breathing and/or cardiopulmonary resuscitation if necessary.
7.   Have victim examined by medical personnel even if victim appears to recover.

Do not...

Leave victim unattended unless absolutely necessary.

AIRWAY OBSTRUCTION

1. Partial obstruction
- Able to inhale some air.
- Coughs forcefully.

Treatment:
- Encourage casualty to cough.
- Do not stop casualty's attempts to free own airway.

2. Complete obstruction

Signs:
- High-pitched or crowing-like noises.
- Unable to breathe or speak.
- Clutches at throat, begins turning blue.
- Increasing weakness.

Treatment:
- Call for help.
- Use the Heimlich manoeuvre:
  – go behind the person, place your arms around her waist;
  – form a fist with one hand, place it thumb-side in, against the victim's abdomen in midline slightly above the navel;
  – grasp the fist with the other hand; and
  – press the fist into the victim's abdomen with a quick upward thrust.
- Repeat above sequence until the victim breathes again.

FROSTBITE

Frostbite is a superficial injury caused by freezing of a small area such as the nose, cheek, fingers or toes.

Symptoms:
- Possible pain or stinging in the frostbite area followed by numbness.
- Area may appear whiter than the surrounding tissue.

Do…
1. Warm the area by steady firm pressure with a warm hand.
2. Blow hot breath on the area.
3. Hold frostbitten area such as fingers against the body (i.e. in armpits).

Do not…
1. Rub frostbitten area.
2. Expose areas to high temperatures.
3. Disturb blisters.

A GIFT OF BLOOD IS A GIFT OF LIFE.

 D Exchange information.

Read one section from pages 76 and 77 carefully. Then, in your own words, explain to students in your group what to do for that injury.

Passive Voice

Use the passive voice with transitive verbs. When the passive voice is used, the **subject** of the sentence is the **recipient** of the action. Compare active and passive sentences.

> Active voice: subject = **doer**
>
> **The secretary** called the next patient.
>
> Passive voice: subject = **recipient**
>
> **The next patient** was called (by the secretary).

To form the passive voice, use the auxiliary verb **be** with the past participle of the main verb. The auxiliary verb indicates the tense (past, present, future). See Appendix 2 on page 149 for a list of irregular past participles.

> Present: The instructions **are written** on the bottle.
>
> Past: The X-ray **was taken** yesterday morning.
>
> Future: The tests **will be done** tomorrow afternoon.

A Give the passive form of the verbs. Use the tense indicated in brackets.

she **tell** (past)   she was told

1. they **admit** (future) to the hospital
2. the regulations **post** (present) by the door
3. a rapid decision **make** (past) by the intern
4. the accident **cause** (past) by the weather
5. blood **pump** (present) through the arteries
6. the man **give** (past) a transfusion
7. that woman **shake up** (present) from the accident
8. the victim **take** (future) by ambulance
9. hospital patients **tell** (present) to stay in bed
10. his operation **perform** (future) tomorrow
11. the cause of the illness **find** (past) with lab tests
12. her leg **break** (past) in a skiing accident
13. a cast **put on** (present) to protect an injury
14. these pills **take** (present) before bedtime
15. that man **see** (future) by a specialist

B   Choose the active or passive form of the verb to complete the sentences. Use the correct tense (past, present, or future).

1.   The accident _____ (cause) by a drunk driver.

2.   An ambulance _____ (take) the victim to the hospital a few minutes ago.

3.   The patient _____ (examine) by the orthopedist soon.

4.   The operation _____ (do) by a surgeon tomorrow.

5.   The nurse _____ (give) a report to the doctor earlier.

6.   Normally, the doors to the examining room _____ (close).

7.   The pediatrician _____ (return) your call later.

8.   The driver of the car _____ (injure) last night.

9.   Generally, patients' charts _____ (keep) in their rooms.

10. Patients' temperatures _____ (take) every four hours.

11. The new medical staff _____ (start) their shift soon.

12. Nothing serious _____ (find) by the tests last week.

13. The results of the test _____ (give) to her tomorrow.

14. The allergist _____ (give) her a shot yesterday.

15. A specialist _____ (call in) by the doctor tomorrow.

THE DOCTOR DIRECTORY

 What is the specialty of each doctor? Work with a partner. Match the doctor to the specialty.

Doctor Directory

1. orthopedist
2. pediatrician
3. radiologist
4. allergist
5. dermatologist
6. cardiologist
7. dentist
8. gerontologist
9. psychiatrist
10. obstetrician
11. hematologist
12. ophthalmologist

a) old age
b) the eyes
c) the skin
d) the mind
e) bones and muscles
f) the teeth
g) allergies
h) pregnancy
i) children
j) X-rays
k) the heart
l) the blood

AT THE MEDICAL CLINIC

LISTENING ACTIVITY 6

A   Look at the picture. What do you think happened to these people?

B   Find these things in the picture:

1. crutches
2. a cane
3. a cast
4. a wheelchair
5. a sling
6. a bandage

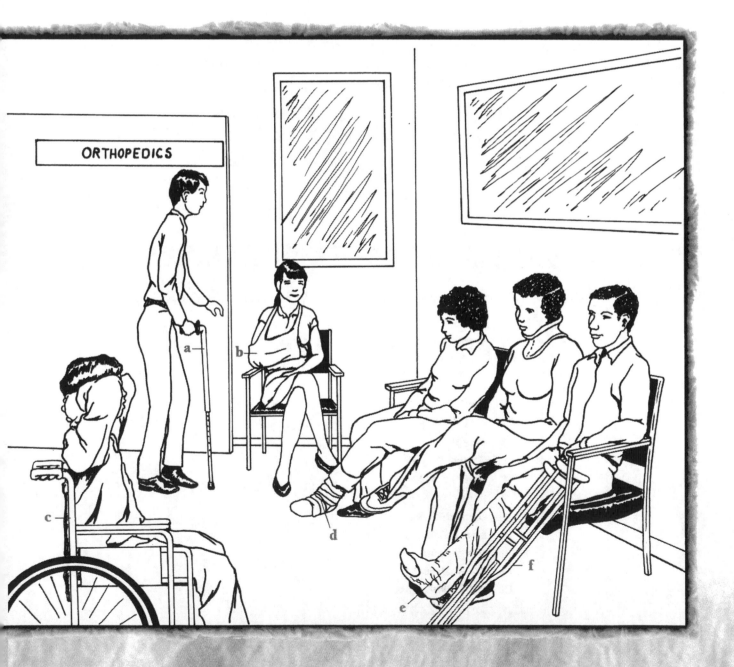

C   Read the questions aloud with a partner.

 D   Listen and answer the questions.

1.   What does the patient think is the problem with her ankle?

2.   How did she get hurt?

3.   How does her ankle look?

4.   What kind of test does the doctor say she needs?

5.   What will she need if the bone is broken?

6.   Why does a sprain sometimes take a long time to heal?

7.   How long will she have to stay off her foot?

8.   How will she get around?

9.   What two things does she have to do to rest her foot?

10.   What does the doctor tell her to do right away?

Turn to page 84 for Exercise E.

ROLE PLAY

Work in pairs. Write a dialogue about going to a medical clinic or a doctor's office.

Act out your dialogue.

THE MEDICINE CABINET

 A   Read the paragraphs. With a partner, discuss what you read and decide what each product is.

1.   Since 1921, people have used more than 100 billion of these. The product was first invented by a man named Earl Dickson, who worked as a cotton buyer for Johnson and Johnson. Mr. Dickson married a woman who was accident-prone, often cutting or burning herself in the kitchen. Until this time, injuries were covered with large surgical bandages. Mr. Dickson set out to devise a small bandage that was easy to apply and would stay clean.

2.   This product is not very old. In fact, it was invented during World War II. At this time, many soldiers went to the Pacific, where they were exposed to the hot sun. The product was invented to prevent them from getting burned. However, this product was not used in a recreational situation until the 1940s, when people began to spend more time at the beach. Until then, people of many cultures had avoided the sun. Pale skin had been the fashion. Today, the letters SPF help us decide which product to buy.

3. People have always used some form of this product. Ancient people used twigs. Later, a small brush was invented, which consisted of animal hairs attached to a bamboo or bone handle. Today, this product is made of plastic, with nylon bristles. It comes in many colours and sizes, and is very inexpensive. Together with a special paste, it helps us keep our smiles white and bright.

4. People in many cultures throughout history have used some form of this product. Cave drawings show that some men used sharp pieces of stone or shell. In some societies, using this product every day was a symbol of status. As sharper instruments were invented, people had to learn how to avoid cutting themselves. Later on, the product became safer to use. Today we can buy several varieties. These include disposable plastic types and electric versions.

5. Long ago, people used a powder from the bark of a tree to help people with a fever. This power contained ingredients that are similar to a product that we use today. Our modern product was invented in Germany in 1899. It was first sold in a powder form, and was available by prescription only. Later it was sold in capsules, and then in tablet form. After almost a century of use, doctors still do not know exactly how it works. However, it is the world's largest selling non-prescription drug.

  B Work with a partner to answer these questions.

1. Which two kinds of products were used in ancient times?
2. Which product is applied to the skin?
3. Which products are made of plastic?
4. Which product is always used outdoors?
5. Which products are used by most people every day?
6. Which product is sold in capsules or tablets?
7. Which product came into use because of a change in fashion?
8. Which products come in many colours?
9. Which product is used even though no one knows how it works?
10. Which product was a status symbol?

JOURNAL

 Write about a medical problem you had, or someone you know had.

PROBLEM SOLVING

What Would You Do?

 Work in groups. Choose what you would do in each situation.

a) Call an ambulance.

b) Go to the emergency ward of a hospital.

c) Go to your doctor or a clinic.

d) Buy an over-the-counter medicine at the drugstore.

e) Use a home remedy. (Explain what it is.)

f) Ask someone for advice. (Who? Your mother, a friend, etc.)

g) Wait and see what happens.

h) Other. (Explain.)

Situations

1.   Your friend falls off a ladder and can't get up.

2.   You twist your ankle while running in the park.

3.   You're having trouble reading the blackboard in class.

4.   You overate at dinner and have a bad stomachache.

5.   You have a cut on your finger that looks infected.

6.   Your cold has turned into a heavy cough that won't go away.

7.   You notice a mysterious rash on your arm.

8.   You are getting a lot of headaches lately.

9.   You have trouble falling asleep at night.

10. You have been feeling depressed recently.

11. Your friend is depressed and won't leave the house.

12. You have a cold with a low fever that has lasted a few days.

13. You have been feeling very irritable and nervous lately.

14. You burn your finger on a hot pot while cooking dinner.

15. You have a severe earache.

16. You have a sore throat.

17. You picked up a heavy box and can't straighten your back.

18. When you run or exercise, you feel a pain in your knee.

19. You stubbed your toe against the door, and it is swollen.

20. You experience pains in your chest and down your arm.

AT THE MEDICAL CLINIC

LISTENING ACTIVITY 6

E   Match the explanations below with the expression in bold.

1. as much as six weeks
2. the hospital will provide you with
3. didn't see
4. I think
5. I'll decide what we should do
6. What is your problem?
7. will be healed
8. be able to move
9. not use your foot
10. take an X-ray

F   Work in pairs. Practise the dialogue with your partner.

Doctor: **What can I do for you?**

Patient: I fell down and hurt my ankle. **I'm afraid** it's broken.

Doctor: How did it happen?

Patient: I was going down the stairs to the basement in my apartment building. It was dark, and I **missed** the last step and fell down.

Doctor: Hmmm. It's a bit swollen and blue. I'm going to examine it. Does it hurt when I press here?

Patient: Ouch! Yeah, a lot.

Doctor: OK, we'd better **get an X-ray** to see if anything is broken.

Patient: Will I need a cast?

Doctor: If the bone is broken, you will. If it's a sprain, we'll put on a bandage.

Patient: If it's just a sprain, it **should be better** in a few days, right?

Doctor: Not necessarily. Sometimes a sprain takes longer to heal than a broken bone. The problem is that people start walking on it before it's healed, and they cause more damage. This looks like a pretty severe sprain. You'll have to **keep off your foot** for a few weeks.

Patient: A few weeks? I didn't know a sprain could last that long.

Doctor: A slight sprain can heal in a few days, but a severe sprain can take **up to six weeks** to heal.

Patient: Oh boy. I thought I'd be OK in a couple of days. How will I **get around**? Do I need crutches?

Doctor: Yes, **we'll give you** crutches. But you'll have to rest your foot as much as you can. Keep your foot on a pillow, and put ice on it to reduce the swelling.

Patient: OK, I understand.

Doctor: Why don't you go to the X-ray department right away? It's on the fourth floor. Then come back to my office and **we'll see what to do next**.

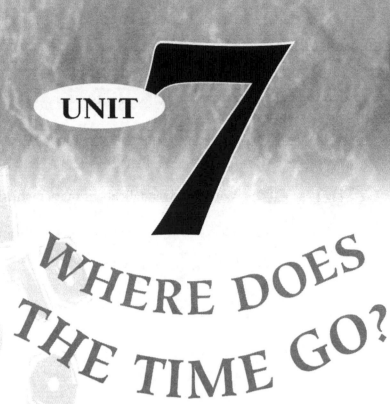

WHERE DOES THE TIME GO?

TIME FLIES

Discuss these statements with your group. Say whether each statement is true or false **for you**.

1. I often feel under stress because I don't have enough time.

2. I'd rather be busy than have a lot of time on my hands.

3. I take some time to relax every day.

4. I usually have enough time to do the things I need to do.

5. Time moves very slowly.

6. Other people seem to manage their time better than I do.

7. I wish I could add _____ hours to my day.

8. I plan to slow down soon.

9. At the end of the day I often feel satisfied about how I spent my time.

10. Time seems to rush by.

THINGS WE DO EVERY DAY

A Work in a group. List some activities you do every day—for example, going to class, preparing food, etc.

B With a partner, talk about the activities listed below. Put the activities into categories. Write the letters for the categories. It is possible for some activities to go in more than one category.

| buying groceries   C |

Categories

A. Household chores

B. Entertainment

C. Food-related activities

D. Grooming

E. Child or pet care

F. Personal/other

Activities

1. buying groceries
2. dusting the furniture
3. showering
4. visiting friends
5. getting a haircut
6. bathing a child
7. washing the kitchen floor
8. brushing your teeth
9. writing a thank-you note
10. washing dishes
11. shopping for clothes
12. taking out the garbage
13. making restaurant reservations
14. cleaning the fridge
15. peeling vegetables
16. exercising
17. cooking a main course
18. going to a doctor's appointment
19. ordering in
20. changing diapers
21. answering the telephone
22. vacuuming the rugs
23. washing your hair

24. going to the dentist
25. visiting a sick relative
26. setting the table
27. reading the newspaper
28. volunteering
29. going to the veterinarian
30. going to a place of worship
31. paying the bills
32. doing sports
33. going to a movie
34. buying a compact disk
35. going to a party
36. watching television
37. taking the car to the garage
38. taking a child to day care
39. doing a hobby
40. reading a bedtime story
41. feeding the dog
42. getting dressed
43. preparing bottles
44. walking the dog
45. sorting laundry

HOW WE SPEND OUR TIME

A   Look at the picture of people doing things. How much time do you think the average person spends on each activity on an average day?

At Home

Sleeping

Personal grooming

Eating at home

Food preparation

Child care

Household chores

Entertainment

Out

At work

In transit

Eating out

Grocery shopping

Exercising

B   Use these estimates to help you. With a partner, copy the chart. Choose an approximate time for each activity listed in the chart. Write the time in the "Estimate" column.

a) 15 minutes or less   d) 1–3 hours

b) 15–30 minutes   e) 3–6 hours

c) 30–60 minutes   f) 7 hours or more

Activities	Estimate	Time
1. working		
2. commuting		
3. grooming		
4. grocery shopping		
5. child care		
6. eating out		
7. eating at home		
8. preparing meals		
9. household chores		
10. pet care		
11. sleeping		
12. entertainment		
13. personal (hobbies, volunteer work, exercising, worship)		
14. other (going to appointments, talking on the phone)		

 C   Read the story about how we spend our time. Then complete the "Time" column in the chart, using the information from the story. When you have finished, compare the actual times on the chart with the times of your estimates.

CANADIAN CAPSULES

Did you know that the average person spends two years of his or her life returning telephone calls?

How We Spend Our Time

How do the majority of Canadians spend their time? Sleeping, working, and watching television. According to recent studies of women and men between 18 and 90 years of age, we also devote a good deal of time to preparing meals and eating, doing household chores, grooming ourselves, travelling to and from activities, and reading or doing hobbies.

So, how much time do we actually spend on each activity? Well, if you owned a mattress company, you would be happy to know that we spend more time sleeping than doing anything else. We spend an average of 7.5 out of every 24 hours sleeping. When awake, we spend the most time in work-related activities— work itself, the time it takes to get ready for work, travelling to and from work, and grooming for work. Full-time workers average about 7.5 hours a day on the job, with an additional 50 minutes per day in transit. Grooming averages another 45 minutes a day.

What do we do in the hours between work and sleep? Entertainment ranks third on the list. About 2.5 hours a day are spent on watching television and videos, listening to music, visiting with friends, or going out for fun. Then there are household chores such as laundry, vacuuming, and dusting. They take about 45 minutes a day.

Of course we have to eat. We spend about two hours a day on food-related activities such as food preparation and eating. Shopping for groceries takes about 15 minutes per day. Preparing food takes about 35 minutes, and eating at home takes about 50 minutes a day. We spend another 25 minutes a day eating out. Then there are other obligations, such as child care and pet care. Child care averages about 1.45 hours a day, with another 20 minutes a day for pet care. Another 45 minutes per day is devoted to personal activities, such as hobbies, exercise, volunteer work, and worship. Everything else, close to three hours a day, falls into a general category, called "other activities." These activities include going to appointments, talking on the telephone, shopping for non-food items, cruising the Internet, or just staring off into space.

These numbers reflect the average "Joe" and "Jane," and do not relate to any specific person. In reality, they vary according to age and lifestyle. A couple with young children devote a much larger portion of their day to child care than do a retired couple. People with full-time jobs spend more time working and in work-related activities than do students or part-time workers. And women and men continue to spend some of their time in different ways.

Interestingly, we seem to be changing the ways we do many activities and the places in which we do them. For example, we spend more time eating and talking on the telephone in cars than we did in the past. And we also eat out, on the run, more than in the past. Perhaps we should add some new categories to the study: Time spent eating on the run? Time spent on the information highway? What about time spent responding to surveys?

D   Work in pairs. Answer the questions **orally**.

1.   Which three activities take up a lot of time for a majority of Canadians?

2.   Which group of people was studied?

3.   Which activity accounts for most of our time?

4.   What is meant by "work-related activities"?

5.   What is the total amount of time spent on work-related activities every day?

6.   How much time is spent on the third and fourth most time-consuming activities?

7.   What is meant by "food-related activities"?

8.   Why are the names "Joe" and "Jane" used?

9.   Give examples of different ways "average times" can vary.

10.   What are three new types of activities that are taking up time today?

E   Match the words that have the same meaning.

1.	chores	a)	free time
2.	leisure	b)	prepare
3.	recently	c)	devote
4.	responsibilities	d)	part
5.	spend (time)	e)	additional
6.	travelling	f)	specific
7.	definite	g)	obligations
8.	the Internet	h)	average
9.	get ready	i)	tasks
10.	extra	j)	lately
11.	typical	k)	transit
12.	portion	l)	the information highway

CANADIAN CAPSULES   In many single-parent families, up to 35 percent of household duties are done by children. These chores include cooking, doing laundry, cleaning, and shopping.

HOW DO YOU SPEND YOUR TIME?

A Look at the time chart for two people, "Joe" and "Jane." Use the example to think about how you spend your time. Draw a circle, and divide it according to your activities.

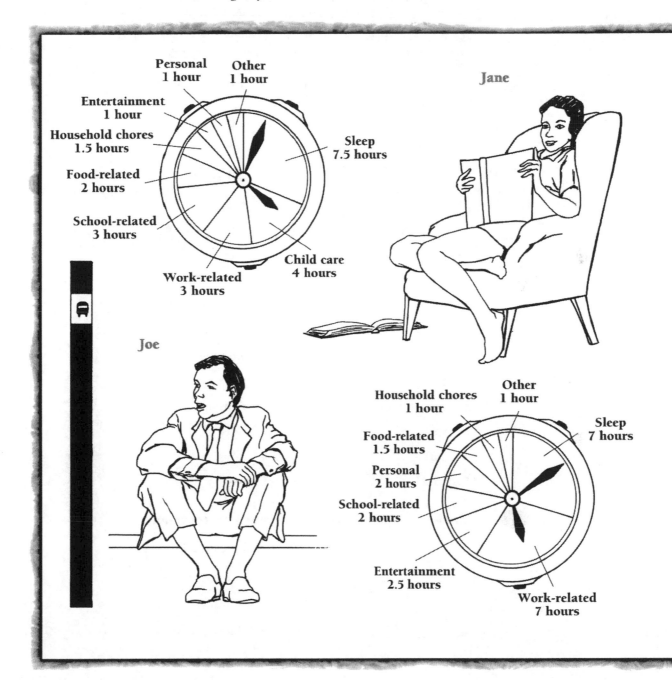

Jane

Personal 1 hour
Other 1 hour
Entertainment 1 hour
Household chores 1.5 hours
Food-related 2 hours
School-related 3 hours
Work-related 3 hours
Child care 4 hours
Sleep 7.5 hours

Joe

Household chores 1 hour
Other 1 hour
Food-related 1.5 hours
Personal 2 hours
School-related 2 hours
Entertainment 2.5 hours
Sleep 7 hours
Work-related 7 hours

B Discuss your charts in a group.

C Survey people in the class. Try to find out who spends the most time sleeping, working, eating, etc.

"How much"/"How many"

Use **how much** to ask WH-information questions about **quantity** with non-count nouns (air, salt). Use **how many** to ask WH-information questions about the **number** of things with count nouns.

> Non-count: How **much** time do you have free?
>
> Count: How **many** hours did you work?

A Work in pairs. Put the following nouns into the count or non-count category. Make lists in your notebook.

1.	days	16.	time
2.	leisure	17.	money
3.	obligations	18.	dollars
4.	travel	19.	exercise
5.	groceries	20.	worship
6.	friends	21.	jobs
7.	furniture	22.	trips
8.	hobbies	23.	laundry
9.	entertainment	24.	fridges
10.	times	25.	garbage
11.	people	26.	pets
12.	information	27.	dentists
13.	tasks	28.	bills
14.	fun	29.	dogs
15.	food	30.	weeks

B Complete the questions with **How much** or **How many**.

1. _____ food do we need to buy?

2. _____ housework is left to do?

3. _____ hours are left in the day?

4. _____ times did the phone ring?

5. _____ kilometres do you walk every day?

6. _____ money did he spend on groceries?

7. _____ things can we do in a day?

8. _____ time does it take to make dinner?

9. _____ effort does it take to watch TV?

10. _____ people helped to cook the meal?

11. _____ luggage did they bring with them?

12. _____ furniture do we need to get?

13. _____ children do you plan to have?

14. _____ meals did you make this week?

15. _____ pets do the children have?

C   Match the non-count nouns with related count nouns.

1.	travel	a)	meals
2.	time	b)	suitcases
3.	clothing	c)	tables
4.	money	d)	shows
5.	furniture	e)	trips
6.	weather	f)	cars
7.	entertainment	g)	blizzards
8.	food	h)	shirts
9.	luggage	i)	dollars
10.	traffic	j)	months

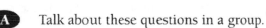

ARRIVING ON TIME

LISTENING ACTIVITY 7

A   Talk about these questions in a group.

1. What does "being on time" mean to you?

2. If you were invited to someone's house for dinner at 6:00, what time would you arrive?

3. How long would you wait for friends before you considered them "late"?

4. How long would you expect friends to wait for you?

B   Read the questions aloud with a partner.

C   Listen and answer the questions.

1.   What time are the students invited for?

2.   What time would they arrive if they met and took the bus at 4:30?

3.   How would the teacher probably feel if the students arrived too early?

4.   In Yumi's culture, when do people arrive for appointments?

5.   What did Elena's neighbour invite her to do?

6.   Why did the neighbour keep looking at her watch?

7.   What did Elena realize?

8.   What time do some of their classmates plan to arrive at the teacher's house?

9.   What does Elena say about being late?

10.   If you are invited somewhere for dinner in Canada, what is a polite time to arrive?

TALK ABOUT IT

Work in a group to discuss these questions.

1.   Did you ever have a problem after arriving too early or too late for an appointment or invitation? What happened?

2.   Did you ever misunderstand another person's concept of time? What happened?

SILENT LETTERS

The following words all contain **silent letters**. Say the words with a partner and decide which letters are not pronounced. Write the words in your notebook and put an **X** through the silent letters.

often	plumber
half	knee
knit	comb
know	salmon
walk	calm
island	knock
answer	lamb
write	listen

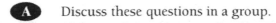

HOLD ON A MOMENT

   VIDEO ACTIVITY 4

   A   Discuss these questions in a group.

1. How much time do you spend waiting in line-ups in a typical week?

2. Where are some of the places where you have to wait in line?

3. How do you feel when you are put on hold when you call someone on the telephone?

4. What do you consider is a reasonable length of time to stay on hold?

5. Do you like to listen to "muzak" when you are on hold?

6. Discuss some good and bad points about "call waiting."

   B   Read the questions aloud with a partner.

   C   Watch the video and answer the questions. Use the worksheet.

1. Who is on the other end of the line when the woman answers the phone?

2. What is the dictionary definition of a "moment"?

3. What are some answers that people give to the question, "How long is a moment?"

4. According to the Bell employee, how long does it take to transfer a call?

5. What does the other man think about having your secretary call someone you want to talk to?

6. How much of our lives do experts say we spend waiting in line-ups?

7. How does one man feel about "muzak"?

8. Which machine has lowered the amount of time we spend waiting in line-ups?

9. Why are some people annoyed by call waiting?

10. According to studies, how long does the average person wait on the telephone before hanging up?

11. How long should it take to return a long-distance call?

12. What do people do when they don't want to wait any longer?

JOURNAL

Write about yourself, and how you spend your time.

PROBLEM SOLVING

What Would You Do?

Work in a group. Discuss and find a solution.

1. You live far from your job or school. You car-pool with a friend who lives in your area and goes in the same direction as you do. You share expenses and take turns driving. The problem is that your friend is frequently late, and you end up waiting. Then you get stuck in traffic and are late for class or work. You don't want to stop the car-pool because it would take much longer to get to work or class by bus.

2. You work or go to class full-time. You always do your grocery shopping and banking on Thursday or Friday evenings or on Saturdays. The problem is that there are long line-ups wherever you go. What can you do to lessen your waiting time?

3. You find that you are frequently late for class or appointments. Although you try to get there on time, for some reason you seldom do. Being late is becoming a habit. What can you do?

4. You usually get to class on time, but several other students generally come in late and disrupt the class. The teacher sometimes waits a few minutes before starting class because she doesn't want to be interrupted during a lesson. What can you suggest?

What Would You Say?

Match the expressions on the left to their meanings on the right.

1.	to kill time	a)	to go slowly
2.	Time flies.	b)	occasionally
3.	It's about time!	c)	to work extra hours
4.	to do overtime	d)	Finally!
5.	once in a blue moon	e)	Time passes quickly.
6.	to take your time	f)	to take a break
7.	to take time off	g)	to waste time

8

IT'S ALL IN THE FAMILY

MARRIAGE TODAY

Read this paragraph. Then close your book and write the paragraph as your teacher dictates it.

Did you know that almost 40 percent of all marriages in North America end in divorce? Some people think that there is something wrong with the way we select our mates. Other people think there may be something wrong with our values. People have many theories about why the rate of divorce is so high, but nobody is sure what the reason is.

TALK ABOUT IT

Discuss these ideas in a group. Which of these are good reasons for getting married?

1. Two people are in love with each other.
2. You are the right age to get married.
3. Most of your friends are married.
4. Your parents suggest you should get married.
5. Your brothers and sisters are married.
6. A person feels really lonely.
7. A woman is over 30 years old.
8. A man is over 30 years old.
9. Both partners have the same interests.
10. Both partners have good jobs.
11. Partners have just bought a house together.
12. Your parents want grandchildren.
13. Two people want to have a family.
14. Your parents know each other well.

ARRANGED MARRIAGE

Complete the paragraph with the words below.

**husband   people   parents   roots   love   families   girl
children   wealth   married**

Arranged marriage has its __1_____ in the past, when marriages were based less on __2_____ and more on the need to build political alliances or to keep __3_____ in the family. In some cases, young __4_____ would be engaged to ensure solid relationships between __5_____. At a time when young people 15 or 16 years old got __6_____, they did not have the life experience to choose a good __7_____ or wife. Then, it was important to have the advice of __8_____. In some cultures today, __9_____ continue to feel that arranged marriage offers a better way of finding a good partner than the "boy meets __10_____" system we have in Canada.

HAPPILY EVER AFTER

A   Work in a group to discuss these questions.

1. Why do so many marriages in North America end in divorce?

2. Is the rate of divorce as high in other countries?

3. Is the rate of unhappy marriages as high in other countries?

4. What would you do if you married someone and then discovered that you were not happy with that person?

5. Do you think that parents have a responsibility to participate in selecting their children's mates?

6. In cultures where people believe parents should participate in selecting children's mates, what arguments do you think they give for doing so?

B   Read and answer the questions **orally** with a partner.

1.   Anil Ghosh studied accounting in Canada and then went to work for the Royal Bank in Toronto. Three years later, at the age of 27, he felt ready to find a wife. The average young man in Canada might date several women before becoming serious enough about one of them to consider marriage. He would be following the custom of "boy meets girl" (you meet someone, fall in love, marry, and live happily ever after). Instead, Ghosh wrote a letter. He was following the custom of his original culture. He wrote to his father in India asking him to arrange a marriage.

2.   Mr. Ghosh Senior asked family, friends, and colleagues for help in finding a young woman. He also placed an ad in the *Times of India*. In the ad he mentioned his son's profession, age, and caste. He also mentioned his first language because there are more than 200 languages in India. He added that the young man spoke English and was established in Canada. As is customary, more than 100 responses came to the post-office box he had rented. The Ghosh family looked through the letters and chose three that seemed to describe suitable young women.

3.   Mr. Ghosh contacted the family of one of the women. With his wife, daughter, and son-in-law, he visited the other family and met the young woman. After the meeting, Mr. Ghosh sent the woman's picture to Canada and the families gave permission to the two young people to exchange letters. Anil wrote about life in Canada. He wanted to be sure his future wife would feel comfortable with the idea of living here. He also made arrangements to go to India on vacation.

4.   Asha Gupta was the young woman chosen to be Anil's future wife. She was a lawyer from the same city as the Ghosh family. She was attractive and healthy and spoke good English. Asha was nervous when Anil first visited her family home. Her parents, two sisters, brother, and sister-in-law were present. Anil came with members of his family too. Asha poured tea and she and Anil chatted about their interests. She liked music and was happy that he played traditional Indian music. He was impressed with her knowledge of Canada and her good English.

5.   Twenty days later the couple married in a traditional Hindu ceremony. They took seven steps around a sacred fire and became husband and wife. Following the wedding, Asha moved to the house of her parents-in-law to wait for the papers she needed to move to Canada to join her new husband. Anil returned to his job in Toronto and began preparing an apartment for the arrival of his bride.

1. What job did Anil Ghosh have in Canada?

2. What does the expression "boy meets girl" mean?

3. Why did Anil write to his father in India?

4. What action did his father take?

5. What did the newspaper ad mention?

6. What did the family do with the responses to the ad?

7. Who accompanied Mr. Ghosh when he visited the young woman's family?

8. What two things happened after the meeting?

9. Why did Anil write about life in Canada in his letters?

10. What job did Asha Gupta have in India?

11. Who was present from Asha's family?

12. What was Asha happy about?

13. What impressed Anil?

14. Describe the marriage ceremony.

15. What did the couple do after the marriage?

C   Work alone. Write answers to the questions.

D   Go back to the story "Happily Ever After." Find words that mean the same as the words below.

Paragraph 1
typical
tradition
first

Paragraph 2
job
settled
appropriate

Paragraph 3
photograph
certain
plans

Paragraph 4
pretty
served
talked

Paragraph 5
marriage
documents
wife

CANADIAN CAPSULES   A nuclear family is made up of parents and their children. An extended family includes parents, children, grandparents, and/or uncles and aunts in the same household.

Conditional I

Use a conditional sentence to show an **if/then** relationship between two actions. Use Conditional I for real future possibility. The **if** clause gives the condition that will make a future action possible.

> If **X** condition is present, then **Y** will happen.

The **if** clause can be first or last without changing the meaning. The **if** is always expressed in **present time**. The **then** clause is always expressed in **future time**.

> If he **proposes** marriage, then she **will accept**.

A   Match the clauses to make logical sentences.

1.	The couple will marry	a)	if our rent goes up again.
2.	They will come for sure	b)	if they didn't eat earlier.
3.	She will become an expert	c)	if there is no entertainment.
4.	We won't wake up in time	d)	if they get an invitation.
5.	Someone will answer the phone	e)	if she doesn't love the man.
6.	She won't marry	f)	if their parents agree.
7.	We will move to another place	g)	if we don't go to bed soon.
8.	They will be hungry	h)	if the weather is good.
9.	They will be bored	i)	if it rings loudly enough.
10.	The wedding will take place outside	j)	if she practises hard enough.

B   Match the clauses to make logical sentences.

1.	If the bus doesn't come soon,	a)	they will cancel the picnic.
2.	If you are the oldest child,	b)	he will probably be an inventor.
3.	If it rains tomorrow,	c)	we will take a taxi.
4.	If there aren't any objections,	d)	they won't get married.
5.	If we don't like the food,	e)	she will probably be a peace maker.
6.	If he is the youngest child,	f)	the children will probably be tall.
7.	If they sleep late,	g)	they will be rested.
8.	If they don't love each other,	h)	you will probably be a leader.
9.	If she is the middle child,	i)	we won't eat it.
10.	If the parents are both tall,	j)	they will be married.

C Put the verbs in the correct tenses.

1. If it _____ (rain), we _____ (need) an umbrella.

2. If no one _____ (be) home, we _____ (come back) later.

3. They _____ (come) for sure if we _____ (invite) them.

4. If you _____(be) too tired, you _____ (not play) well.

5. You _____ (not find) parking if you _____ (arrive) late.

6. Their parents _____ (agree) to the marriage if their children _____ (be) in love.

7. If she _____ (fall) in love, she _____ (marry).

8. If the couple _____(be) happy, the parents _____ (be) happy.

9. We _____ (use) a parking lot if there _____ (be) no parking spot on the street.

10. We _____ (invite) them if you _____ (give) us their address.

FAMILY LIFE

Work in a group to discuss these questions.

1. Do you come from a big family or a small family?

2. How many brothers or sisters do you have?

3. Is this considered a big, average,or small family in your culture?

4. What is your position in the family?

5. What were some household chores when you were growing up (washing the dishes, sweeping the floor, making the beds)?

6. Who did them?

7. Who did the cooking in your family?

8. What responsibilities did you have in the family?

A PLACE IN THE FAMILY

LISTENING ACTIVITY 8

A   Work alone. Think about **yourself**. First, choose your position in the family. Then choose the characteristics that you think are **true for you**. Use the list below to help you. Add any other characteristics you can think of.

Position in family

In my family, I am the:

a) first-born

b) middle child

c) youngest child

d) only child

Characteristics

1. good sense of humour

2. loyal

3. easy going

4. serious

5. ambitious

6. creative

7. a natural entertainer

8. responsible

9. good leader

10. problem-solver

11. get along well with others

12. practical

13. shy

14. outgoing

15. hard working

16. relaxed

17. other (Explain.)

B   Exchange information.

Find at least two other students in the class who have the same position in the family.

Compare your information. How many characteristics are the same? How many are different?

After you have finished, compare your information with that of other groups.

C Read the statements aloud with a partner. Discuss and choose the answers that you think are correct.

1. According to experts, our place in the family:

   a) can make a difference to our personalities

   b) doesn't make much difference to our personalities

2. Youngest children generally:

   a) are natural entertainers

   b) don't like to perform in public

3. Youngest children are often:

   a) creative

   b) practical

4. The majority of scientific discoveries in the last five years were made by:

   a) youngest children

   b) oldest children

5. Oldest children are generally:

   a) easy-going

   b) serious

6. A good career for a first-born would be:

   a) a social worker

   b) a journalist

7. All of the astronauts in the U.S. space program have been:

   a) first-borns

   b) middle children

8. Middle children are generally good at:

   a) taking responsibility

   b) solving problems

9. Middle children are attracted to careers as:

   a) managers

   b) teachers

10. Experts say that birth order:

   a) can tell you what kind of career a person will have

   b) is only part of the picture

D   Listen to check your answers.

   E   In a group, talk about what you heard. How close are you to the "typical" first-born, middle child, or youngest child? In which ways are you different?

PRESENTATION

Prepare a five-minute presentation about a traditional get-together in your family. It can be a birthday celebration, New Year celebration, anniversary, or any other time your family meets. Talk about who is there, what you eat, special clothes you wear, and special things you do.

JOURNAL

Write about a traditional family get-together. Use ideas from the presentation to help you.

PROBLEM SOLVING

What Would You Do?

Work in groups. Discussion the situations below. What would you do? Who could you ask for help?

For help

a) a doctor

b) a teacher

c) a social worker

d) the police

e) a friend

f) your parents

g) your sister/brother

h) other

Situations

1. You have moved to a new city and don't know many people. You feel very lonely and you want to make new friends.

2. Your child or younger sibling is being bullied by some big kids in the school yard.

3. You think that a child in your building is being neglected or abused by his or her parents.

4. Someone in your family has lost his or her job and is angry or depressed.

5. You think that the woman who lives next door to you is being abused because you hear a lot of screaming and loud noises.

6. You suspect that your daughter or younger sister has been shoplifting because you notice a lot of things in her room that you know she can't afford.

7. You would like to get married, and want to meet a nice young man or woman.

8. Your parents want you to get married, but you are not ready to settle down.

9. You are married. Your parents tell you all the time that they want grandchildren, but you are not ready to have children.

10. Your brother doesn't have a job and is not trying very hard to get one. You have a job and work very hard. Now your brother wants to come and live with you.

11. You share an apartment with a roommate. Your roommate eats a lot of the food you buy and prepare, but doesn't replace it or cook very much. You feel your roommate is taking advantage of you.

12. You are looking for a roommate and don't know where to find one.

13. You are having trouble in your marriage and need counselling.

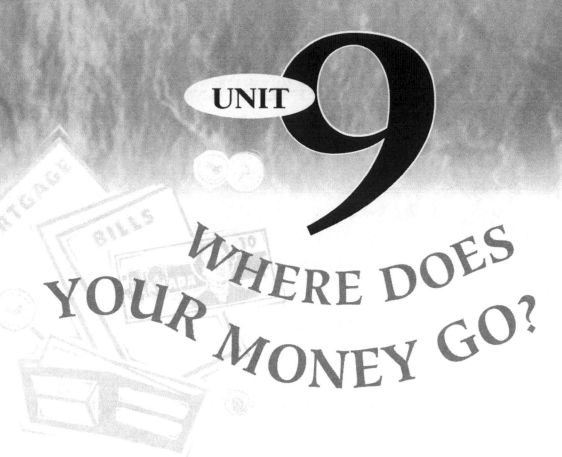

UNIT 9

WHERE DOES YOUR MONEY GO?

BANKING

Discuss these questions in a group.

1. Do you have a bank account?

2. Do you have a bank card?

3. What does PIN stand for?

4. Why is it important not to tell anyone else your PIN?

5. What transactions do you usually do with your bank card?

6. Have you ever paid a bill at the automatic teller?

7. What else can you do with a bank card (besides use the automatic teller)?

PAYING THE PHONE BILL

LISTENING ACTIVITY 9

A   Read the questions aloud with a partner.

B   Listen and answer the questions.

1. When did Janet go to the bank?

2. Why was she upset?

3. Why does Paula think the bank was so crowded that day?

4. Why doesn't Janet usually have to wait when she goes to the bank?

5. Why didn't she go to the automatic teller today?

6. Why is Janet surprised?

7. What two ways does Paula suggest for learning about the automatic teller?

8. Which way does Janet think she will choose?

9. What suggestion does Paula make?

10. How will Paula and Janet get together after work?

Turn to page 120 for Exercise C.

HOW TO USE AN AUTOMATIC TELLER

A   Read the text quickly. Then close your book and write while the teacher dictates.

> In the past, when we needed money, we went to our bank and withdrew money from our savings or chequing account. Then we used cash to buy the things we needed. Most daily purchases were paid for in cash. Bills for electricity, heating, or telephone services were paid by cheque. So was the rent. Cash and cheques are still used today, but there are new ways of doing banking now. More and more people are withdrawing money and paying bills at the automatic teller.

CANADIAN CAPSULES

The words "saving money" are used in different ways in Canada. When bankers talk about saving money, they mean keeping money in the bank. But when stores talk about saving money, they mean that you can buy something at a lower price.

B Work with a partner. Put the steps for withdrawing cash in the correct order.

1. Wait; your request is being processed.

2. Remove your card.

3. Select an account.

4. Enter your PIN and press OK.

5. Remove your cash and transaction record.

6. Insert your card as shown.

7. Select a transaction.

8. Select the amount of money you want.

WHAT DO YOU MEAN?

Match the terms below to the meanings.

1.	fare	a)	money you borrow
2.	a deposit	b)	money you take from the bank
3.	tuition	c)	money parents give children weekly
4.	an allowance	d)	money you owe
5.	a buck	e)	money you pay for studies
6.	a tip	f)	money from your employer
7.	a withdrawal	g)	money you put in the bank
8.	a salary	h)	money you pay for transportation
9.	a loan	i)	one dollar
10.	a debt	j)	money for good service

CANADIAN CAPSULES The three top expenditures by an average Canadian family are—in order—personal taxes, shelter, and food. Transportation is the next largest outlay, followed by clothing, recreation, and household operating costs.

Present Perfect Aspect for Duration of Time

Use the present perfect for an action that began in the past and continues in the present.

> Are you a customer at this branch?
>
> Yes. I **have been** a customer here for eight years.

To form the present perfect, use the auxiliary verb **have** + the past participle of the main verb. Use the third person singular form **has** with the subjects **she**, **he** or **it**.

A   Complete the sentences with the present perfect form of the verb.

1. Mrs. Smith _____ (be) a customer here for many years.

2. That teller _____ (work) at this branch for ages.

3. I _____ (know) that bank manager for many years.

4. The automatic tellers _____ (be) out of order all morning.

5. They _____ (live) in this neighbourhood longer than Bob.

6. Some employees _____ (go) home early for the weekend.

7. Antonio _____ (have) an account here since last year.

8. Junko _____ (speak) English since she was a child.

9. This branch _____ (be) open since last September.

10. I _____ (have) a bank card since I opened my account.

B   Choose the **simple past** (for completed actions) or the **present perfect** (for actions that began in the past and continue in the present).

1. Karen _____ (work) at the bank before she got married.

2. Carlos _____ (live) here since he got his new job.

3. Geoff _____ (speak) Japanese since he worked in Kyoto.

4. Liz _____ (speak) French to the travel agent in Paris.

5. Jan and Ben _____ (work) all through last weekend.

6. Suki _____ (be) a customer here for many years.

7. Vera _____ (know) Tamara since they were young.

8. Marc _____ (have) an account here longer than I have.

9. Po-ling _____ (work) as a teller since she arrived here.

10. Paolo _____ (have) two bank accounts in Switzerland.

Present Perfect: Questions Related to Duration of Time

When the present perfect is used for duration of time, the expression **long** or **how long** is often used.

> Have you been here **long**? No, just five minutes.
>
> **How long** has she worked here? About two years.

A Read the sentences. Write questions to help you get more information. Use **how long** and the present perfect.

1. Ping lives in Vancouver.

2. He goes to a technical college.

3. Ping's uncle and aunt have a grocery store.

4. Ping works in the store on weekends.

5. He knows a young woman from Toronto.

6. They are in the same class.

7. She speaks Mandarin.

8. Her family lives in London.

9. She works in the library after school.

10. Ping and the young woman are good friends.

Present Perfect: Negative

The most common uses of the present perfect negative when it is related to duration of time are for short answers in denials or for contradictions.

> **Denial:** Have you been here long? No, I **haven't.**
>
> **Contradiction:** She **hasn't** worked here for a month.
>   She has worked here for a year.

A Write six questions to ask your partner. Use the present perfect and the verbs **be**, **work**, **have**, **know**, **live**, **go to school**, **speak a language**.

 B Ask your questions. Answer your partner's questions with the short answer form **Yes, I have** or **No, I haven't**.

MAKING MONEY

A   Make a chart similar to the one below. Put these words into the appropriate categories. Follow the example.

private detective	son	daughter
fake	bills	false
banknotes	counterfeit	engraver
father	enterprise	factory
illegal	currency	money dealer
dishonest	company	crooked

Jobs	private detective		
Relationships			
Money			
Business			
Not real			
Wrong			

B   Read the questions and find the answers in the text. Discuss the answers **orally** with a partner.

1. Name two things in which farm families have traditionally shared.
2. Give three examples of family enterprises.
3. When and where did the Johnson family go into business?
4. What was their business?
5. What did the father do in the family business?
6. What did the daughters do?
7. What did the sons do?
8. What did the mother do?
9. Why was the Johnson family business illegal?
10. What had they done by the time they were caught?
11. Give three examples of "get-rich-quick" schemes.
12. When do people often buy lottery tickets?
13. How much do Canadians spend on lottery tickets each year?
14. What are sweepstakes?
15. Is it possible to win a lot of money on the sweepstakes?
16. What is the old-fashioned way of making money?

Making Money

In all cultures, it has always been a tradition for families to get together to make money. Farm families everywhere divide up the chores and share in the profits. Trades have been passed from father to son or from mother to daughter at various times in human history. Factories, circuses, and small business have been family enterprises too.

At the end of the last century, one family in Toronto, Ontario, found an unusual enterprise. In the 1880s, the Johnson family decided to make money—literally. It happened like this. Mr. Johnson was an engraver who decided to go into the business of making money. He began to work at engraving plates that looked like Canadian currency. The daughters in the family forged the signatures of government officials on the bills. The sons then printed copies of the fake bank notes. Finally, Mrs. Johnson sold the bills to a dishonest money dealer.

Because the Canadian criminal code forbids illustrating, photographing, or reproducing any part of a real bank note, the Johnson family enterprise was illegal. Making false money is known as counterfeiting, and it got the family into trouble with the law. A private investigator was hired to find the source of the counterfeit money. By the time he caught up with the Johnsons, however, they had printed and put into circulation more than $1 million dollars in fake currency.

Get-rich-quick schemes have always been a dime a dozen. And some of them are even legal: discover a gold mine, crack the lottery system, follow the advice of an investment newsletter, marry a millionaire, become a movie star or a television faith healer, invent a new computer chip or a better mousetrap. Someone, somewhere has struck it rich on such ventures.

If you can't find a good scheme for making money quickly, you can always hope to win money. People line up at the lottery ticket booths on pay day in hopes of winning big bucks. It is estimated that Canadians shell out some $2.5 billion annually for lottery tickets. And while fewer than 10 percent of Canadians participate in the stock market, seven billion shares with a value of $58 billion were traded on Canadian stock exchanges last year. Clearly, some people are trying to make money quickly.

Then there are the sweepstakes—those notices that arrive in your mail telling you that you may already be the winner of a large cash prize, and that all you have to do to claim your

prize is follow instructions. These may consist of buying a magazine or product or calling a special number, so that you will be eligible for the grand prize. Are these sweepstakes legal? Well, some are, and some aren't. Can you actually win big money? You may win money, but it may be less than you think.

If you really want to have a lot of money, you may have to do it the old-fashioned way—earn it. As the Canadian newspaper tycoon Roy Thompson once said, "I am willing to do anything for money, even work."

C Answer the questions in writing. Use your notebook.

SWEEPSTAKES

VIDEO ACTIVITY 5

The word "sweepstakes" means a race or contest in which the complete prize is given to one winner. Have you ever received a sweepstakes envelope, saying that you could win a lot of money? What did you do?

    A   Read the questions aloud with a partner.

    B   Watch the video and answer the questions. Use the worksheet.

1. What do the sweepstakes letters say?

2. What are some things people dream of doing if they win the sweepstakes?

3. How much does the letter say winners could receive?

4. What is the per-minute charge to find out what you have won?

5. How old do you have to be to be eligible for the prize?

6. What is the average time of a call?

7. What information does the man enter first?

8. What is the answer to the skill-testing question?

9. How much time does the man have to answer the question?

10. How long has he been on the phone at this point?

11. What does his 9-digit identification number have to match?

12. How much money will he receive?

13. What number do you press if you don't have children under 18?

14. What number should you press if you rent your home?

15. Which number should you press if you don't have a bank card?

16. Which number should you press if you made a purchase from a general merchandise catalogue?

17. How long has the man been on the phone now?

18. How much does the call cost?

19. How much money was the cheque for?

TALK ABOUT IT

Work in a group to discuss these questions.

1. How much money do you need to be happy?

2. How much money does someone need to be rich?

3. If you won a lot of money, how would you spend it?

JOURNAL

Describe your feelings about money. Use the questions above to help you.

PROBLEM SOLVING

What Would You Say or Do?

Work in a group to discuss these situations. What would you say or do in each case?

1. You think someone in your class stole your wallet, but you aren't sure.

2. You buy something in a store and the cashier gives you an extra dollar in your change.

3. You took out a student loan and are having trouble paying it back.

4. You forgot to pay your phone bill, and received a letter saying your phone services will be cut.

5. You've lost your bank card.

6. You take a taxi and realize that you have just enough money to pay the fare, but not enough for a tip.

7. You receive a notice in the mail saying that your name has been selected to win a big prize.

8. Someone calls you on the phone and asks for your charge card number so that you can be eligible for a prize.

9. You wrote a cheque for your rent, but afterwards you realized that there was not enough money in your account to cover the cheque.

10. Your friend frequently borrows money from you and forgets to pay it back.

11.   Your classmates like to go out to eat a few times a week, but you don't have enough money to eat out more than once a week.

12.   You always buy your friend a nice birthday gift, but he or she buys you something small and inexpensive.

13.   You eat in a restaurant with a friend. Your friend orders an expensive meal. Your meal is not expensive. Then your friend wants to split the cost of the meal.

14.   You find a wallet in the street that has a lot of money. This money could really help you because you have a lot of debts.

15.   You notice that a store made a mistake on your bill. Instead of charging you $17, they charged you $7.

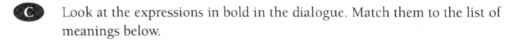

PAYING THE PHONE BILL

LISTENING ACTIVITY 9

C   Look at the expressions in bold in the dialogue. Match them to the list of meanings below.

1.   What a surprise!

2.   I would like to

3.   I think

4.   It seems like a good idea.

5.   not having enough time

6.   I had to wait a long time.

7.   Come with me.

D   Practise the dialogue in pairs.

Paula: You look upset Janet. What happened?

Janet: Oh, I'm just frustrated Paula. I went to the bank at lunch hour to pay my phone bill. I had to wait in line for 35 minutes. I almost didn't have time for lunch. I hate **being rushed**.

Paula: It's pay day in a lot of companies today. **I guess** that's why the bank was so crowded.

Janet: Yeah. Usually I use the automatic teller to withdraw money. I go to the machine after work and I never have to wait. But today I had to pay the phone bill so **I was stuck in this line**. I wish I could pay bills at the machine too.

Paula: Janet, you can pay bills at the machine!

Janet: **You're kidding!** I didn't know that. How do you know what to do?

Paula: You have a choice. The bank has a pamphlet that explains how to do different transactions at the automatic teller, or you can ask one of the tellers at the bank to show you what to do. I pay all my bills at the machine.

Janet: I think I'll pick up a pamphlet next time I'm in the bank. **I wouldn't mind** using the automatic teller. It sure beats waiting in line.

Paula: Say, I have an idea. I have to pay some bills after work. You can **come along** and I'll show you how the machine works if you like.

Janet: **That sounds good.** Let's meet at the front door after work.

Paula: OK. See you later.

JOBS, JOBS, JOBS

  A Work with a partner. Match the kind of work with the workplace.

If you need help, use a dictionary.

1.	chef	a)	a garage
2.	an artist	b)	an airplane
3.	a reporter	c)	a hospital
4.	a mechanic	d)	an apartment building
5.	a farmer	e)	a school
6.	a pilot	f)	a swimming pool
7.	a lifeguard	g)	a restaurant
8.	an orderly	h)	a radio station
9.	a caretaker	i)	a salon
10.	a hairdresser	j)	a barn
11.	a disk jockey	k)	a newspaper
12.	a principal	l)	a studio

B   Match the expressions to the meanings.

1.	a job opening	a)	a list of your duties
2.	to be laid off	b)	a personnel (human resources) officer
3.	to be hired	c)	a candidate asking for a job
4.	prior work history	d)	a position that is available
5.	job skills	e)	letters from former employers
6.	to get fired	f)	jobs you have done in the past
7.	references	g)	tasks that you are trained to do
8.	a recruiter	h)	to get a job
9.	an applicant	i)	to lose a job due to lack of work
10.	a job description	j)	to lose a job as a result of poor performance

TALK ABOUT IT

Discuss these questions in a group.

1. Do you work now?
2. If you work now, how did you get the job?
3. Have you had a job in the past?
4. If you worked in the past, how did you get the jobs you had?
5. Do you remember your first job?
6. Name five different jobs you like and explain why you like them.

THE JOB SEARCH

A   Work in a group. Think about looking for a job in Canada. Discuss the statements below. Decide if each one is a "Do" or a "Don't."

1. Spend time getting documents and papers together.
2. Look for an employer who doesn't require a SIN.
3. Make an application for one job at a time.
4. Sleep in so you will be rested before you start your hunt.
5. Check the yellow pages for companies that need your skills.
6. Make newspaper ads your main source of information.
7. Ask for information about job training at a Canada Employment Centre.

8. Let family and friends know you are looking for a job.

9. Tell people such as your dry cleaner that you are looking for a job.

10. Be direct when you ask for help finding a job.

 B Read and check your answers.

The Job Search

Looking for a job can be an exciting experience that offers new opportunities. It can also be frustrating and discouraging. Most of us will have the experience of looking for a job at least a few times in our lives, so some tips are useful. Employment counsellors suggest that good job hunting strategies can be very useful. They suggests some "Dos" and "Don'ts" for finding a job.

First you should think about documents you need. For example, educational diplomas, degrees, and certificates of competence should be translated into English or French. A curriculum vitae is important to show your education and work history. The most important document a person needs to work in Canada is a social insurance card, because employers are required by law to ask for it. Canadian citizens and landed immigrants can apply for their cards at Canada Employment Centres.

To begin your job search, make a list of the jobs you are qualified to do. Then find out what is available in your area. Check the Yellow Pages directory to get information about companies that might need your skills. Apply even if these companies are not advertising for help. Many companies have openings that are not advertised. Apply to as many places as possible to increase your chances for success.

Canada Employment Centres are operated by the federal government. They have lists of jobs, both locally and in different parts of the country. Counsellors can offer advice about job hunting. They can also help with information about training programs and language courses.

The classified section of the newspaper can be useful too, but beware of ads that promise amazing opportunities with a small investment. Ads like that often lead people to lose their money.

Although advertisements are useful, employment counsellors say they are not the best source of jobs. They recommend networking, pointing out that between 40 and 70 percent of the jobs people get come from personal contacts. Counsellors advise you to tell your family, friends, and people in your neighbourhood, such as your dry cleaner, that you are looking for a job. Be direct. Say something like, "Do you know of any jobs available in (my field)?" You never know who will have a tip for you.

Finally, be flexible. Don't rule out jobs that might be a second or third choice. If you get your foot in the door, other jobs may become available later. Temporary jobs often end up as permanent jobs, since companies are more likely to offer permanent jobs to people they already know than to take a chance on an unknown.

If an employer is interested in hiring you, you will have to go for a job interview. Successful candidates are the ones who are well prepared, and who make a good impression.

C   Read carefully and answer the questions below in writing.

1.   What are two kinds of experiences you can have looking for a job?
2.   Why are good job-hunting strategies useful to most people?
3.   Who suggests "Dos" and "Don'ts" for job hunting?
4.   What documents should be in English or French?
5.   What does a curriculum vitae show?
6.   What do you need before an employer can hire you?
7.   Where can you get a social insurance card?
8.   What information can you get from the Yellow Pages?
9.   Why should you apply if the companies are not advertising?
10.   What information can you get at Canada Employment Centres?
11.   What kind of information can counsellors give you?
12.   What can happen if you answer ads that ask for money?
13.   Why do counsellors recommend networking?
14.   Give some examples of personal contacts that are suggested.
15.   Why is it a good idea to take a second or third choice, or a temporary job?
16.   What two things lead to success in a job interview?

THE FORMAL APPLICATION

A   Almost everybody who has a job has gone through the process of making applications. Generally, people go through the process quite a few times before they find a job they like. Formal job applications are the first contact with your future employer and they can pave the way to a job interview.

Look at the cover letter and résumé on pages 127–129. Give the following information about the applicant.

1.   name, address, and telephone number of one referee
2.   educational background
3.   skills, interests, and hobbies
4.   reasons why an employer should hire the person
5.   name and address of the last employer
6.   volunteer or community work
7.   type of work done in the past
8.   cities in which the person has worked
9.   languages spoken
10.   training in progress

2473 Maplewood, #205
Toronto, Ontario
M1P 2J7

June 12, 199_

Dear Sir/Madam,

Please accept this application for the position of sales clerk which was advertised in the *Toronto Star* on Thursday. I feel that I have the qualifications you require. My curriculum vitae gives details of my education and experience. I have a high-school education, and I speak three languages: English, French, and Portuguese.

My work experience has not been in department stores, but I have worked as a sales clerk in both Vancouver and Toronto.

I am well organized and punctual. I enjoy meeting the public and I liked my previous jobs. I feel that my enthusiastic manner and friendly personality would make me a good candidate to work in the sportswear department of your store.

I am available for an interview at your convenience. If I am hired, I can begin work immediately.

If you require further information about my past performance, please feel free to contact the people named in my CV. Thank you for your consideration.

Yours sincerely,

Gerry Pinto

Gerry Pinto

CURRICULUM VITAE

Gerry Pinto

Address   2473 Maplewood, #205
                           Toronto, Ontario
                           M1P 2J7
                           (416) 392-1546

SIN   221 786 724

Languages   English, Portuguese, French

EDUCATION
1994   Certificate of Recreation
                           Vancouver Community College

1992   Certificat en français, langue seconde
                           UBC Summer School of French

1990   High School Diploma
                           Oak Bay High School
                           Victoria, BC

JOB EXPERIENCE
April 1995–present   Antonio's Sporting Goods
                           North York Mall, Toronto

                           My duties are serving customers, operating
                           the cash register, stocking the shelves, and
                           making minor repairs to bicycles.

May 1992–
January 1995   Vancouver Book Exchange
                           Granville Street, Vancouver

                           I was responsible for serving customers,
                           unpacking books and placing them on the
                           shelves, shipping orders, and labelling
                           merchandise.

–2–

Sept. 1990–July 1992   Burnaby Saddle Shop
                            Wentworth Street, Vancouver

                            My job was serving customers, taking orders
                            by phone from stores we sold to, and
                            cleaning up the store and work room.

ACTIVITIES

I was involved with coaching junior tennis in the Vancouver Parks
programme, and I am now teaching swimming at the Community
Recreation Centre in Scarborough as a volunteer.

I enjoy recreational bicycle riding, camping, and hiking.

I am presently taking a course in bookkeeping at Seneca College.

REFERENCES

Ms Jean Wei, Manager
Antonio's Sporting Goods
North York Mall
1764 Bishop Street
Toronto, ON
M2G 1J6
(416) 343 9660

Mr. Tony Green, Coordinator
Community Outreach Project
Community Recreation Centre
Scarborough, ON
M4P 1Y6
(416) 293 3648

Mr. Jack McKenzie, Owner
Burnaby Saddle Shop
1826 Wentworth Street
Vancouver, BC
V4T 6J8
(604) 277 2204

B   Work with a partner. Choose one of the ads below. Prepare a résumé and an appropriate cover letter.

SHOE SALES
Shoe salesperson required for children's shoes. Exp. pref.
785-3824

WAITER/WAITRESS,
steak and seafood restaurant in Oakville.
Must be experienced in tableside service.
Fax résumé: 487-0916

TRAINEES
Giftware manuf. needs sales trainees. Starting salary $350 wk. no exp.
665-9768

Couriers:
cars or bikes.
Good earnings.
Own vehicle.
921-7689

RECEPTIONIST
for dental office,
441-6779

CASHIER for supermarket.
Exper. Call Mary:
870-6512

 **GRAMMAR FOCUS**   "Have to"/"Don't have to"/"Must not"

Use **have to** to express obligations or actions that are necessary for you to take.

> Stan **has to** be at work by eight o'clock. (It's a company rule.)
>
> I **have to** go to bed soon. (I'm really tired.)

Use **don't have to** for lack of necessity.

> We **don't have to** wear winter clothes today. (It's warm out.)
>
> He **doesn't have to** be back until 1:10. (The rules aren't very strictly enforced.)

To form a sentence with **have to** or **don't have to**, use the expressions (**have to** or **has to**; **don't have to** or **doesn't have to**) followed by the base form of the main verb.

A   Complete the sentences with the correct form of **have to**.

1.   A job applicant _____ arrive on time for an interview.

2.   Workers _____ punch in before they start their shifts.

3.   The public _____ pay to park in the underground garage.

4.   All male employees _____ wear suits and ties to work.

5. Simon _____ pass probation before he becomes permanent.

6. Someone _____ answer the phone by the third ring.

7. People who apply here _____ be ready to work hard.

8. She _____ have at least three years experience to apply.

9. We _____ finish all our work before we leave the office.

10. Li _____ bring a note from the doctor to get paid for time off.

11. I _____ have a clean desk or I can't work properly.

12. The sales representative _____ make a bi-weekly report.

13. Everyone _____ file an income tax report every year.

14. We all _____ attend the sales meeting on Wednesday.

15. The coffee machine _____ be turned off before we leave.

B Complete the sentences with the correct form of **don't have to**.

1. Mike is happy because he _____ go to work today.

2. People in our office _____ be at work until 9:00.

3. Secretaries _____ make coffee in this office.

4. The sales representative _____ call her manager every day.

5. The manager _____ consult all the employees.

6. I _____ finish the annual sales report today.

7. These new machines _____ be serviced very often.

8. The security guard _____ work all night.

9. The mail _____ be delivered before ten o'clock.

10. New employees _____ work double shifts this week.

11. The nurses in this ward _____ wear uniforms anymore.

12. They _____ hand in their expense sheet until next week.

13. I _____ file these legal documents. You do.

14. The lawyer _____ be in court tomorrow.

15. The company _____ hire any new employees this month.

CANADIAN CAPSULES

It is illegal in Canada for an employer to ask your age or religion.

C   Choose **mustn't** (to express prohibitions or warnings) or **don't have to** (to express lack of necessity). Complete the sentences with the verbs in brackets.

1. They lock the door at 10:30. We _____ our keys. (forget)

2. Visitors and customers _____ their passes. (carry)

3. The traffic is terrible. You _____ the street in the middle of the block. (cross)

4. Ben exercises every day. He _____ about his weight. (worry)

5. This is a "no parking" zone. You _____ here before six. (park)

6. July 1 is a civic holiday. We _____ to work today. (go)

7. When the fire bell rings, people _____ in the building. (stay)

8. The boss speaks French well. He _____ a translator. (have)

9. The rules here are strict. We _____ late for work. (be)

10. If you haven't read the contract, you _____ it. (sign)

11. When you leave the factory, you _____ to lock up. (forget)

12. If you have a contract, you _____ about your job. (worry)

13. If you get an interview, you _____ late. (arrive)

14. Employees _____ on vacation without signing out. (leave)

15. They _____ to thank the speaker after the meeting. (forget)

FIRST IMPRESSIONS

A   Discuss these questions in a group.

1. Have you ever been interviewed for a job?

2. What kind of job was the interview for?

3. Where was the interview?

4. Who was present?

5. What kind of questions were asked?

6. What would you do differently in another interview?

B   In a group, read and discuss the questions. Choose the best answers.

1. You should go to a job interview:
    a) alone   c) with a family member
    b) with a friend

2. If you are called for an interview at ten o'clock, you should arrive:
    a) ten minutes early   c) ten minutes late
    b) right on time

3. When the interviewer greets you, you should:
    a) Say "Hi!"   c) ask his or her name
    b) smile and shake hands

4. If you are a smoker and need a cigarette during the interview, you should:
    a) ask if the interviewer minds if you smoke
    b) offer the interviewer a cigarette too
    c) refrain from smoking during the interview

5. The best answer to, "Why do you want this job?" is:
    a) "I really need the money at the moment."
    b) "I feel I could do a good job for this company."
    c) "I've heard this company has good benefits."

6. When the interviewer asks questions, you should:
    a) go into lots of detail
    b) answer briefly with "yes" or "no"
    c) answer as directly as you can

7. If you feel nervous during the interview, it is a good idea to:
    a) tell a joke to warm up the atmosphere
    b) concentrate on your answers to the questions
    c) mention that you really need the job

8. If the interviewer asks your age, you should say:
    a) "I'd rather not discuss my age."
    b) "It's none of your business."
    c) "I'm 46. How about you?"

9. If you are kept waiting for an interview, you should:
    a) go out for coffee and come back later
    b) clear your throat loudly a few times
    c) read a book or magazine while you wait

10. When the interview is over, you should:
    a) ask if you got the job
    b) say you really want the job
    c) say "thank you" to the interviewer

THE JOB INTERVIEW

LISTENING ACTIVITY 10

A   Read the questions aloud with a partner.

B   Listen and answer the questions.

1.   Which job is Barbara applying for?

2.   Where did Barbara work before?

3.   For how long did she work there?

4.   Where did she work before that?

5.   Why did she leave her last job?

6.   What kind of education does she have?

7.   What personality characteristics make her suitable for this job?

8.   What kind of information does Barbara ask for?

9.   What kind of work would Barbara do in this job?

10.   Why are there good chances for promotion with this company?

11.   When will the interviewer contact her?

Turn to page 136 for Exercise C.

FOCUS ON LANGUAGE: HOMONYMS

Work with a partner. Choose the correct word to complete the sentence.

1. This job would be easier if they could **hire/higher** more people.

2. The news about the company's losses upset the **hole/whole** staff.

3. Nobody **guest/guessed** that she was the manager of a large hotel.

4. The receptionist said the cheque was already in the **male/mail**.

5. The director is a person with high moral **principles/principals**.

6. Before the meeting begins, someone has to call the **role/roll**.

7. The customer gave the sales clerk a **piece/peace** of her mind.

8. The person with the best sales record **won/one** an award.

9. Customers don't like it if they have to **weight/wait** too long.

10. The manager thought the coffee **brakes/breaks** were too long.

11. Everyone in the office worked hard to **meat/meet** the deadline.

12. The accountant said **our/hour** pay cheques would be ready on time.

ROLE PLAY

Work in pairs. Write a dialogue about a job interview. Act it out.

PROBLEM SOLVING

What Would You Say or Do?

Work in a group to discuss these situations. What would you say or do in each of the following cases?

1. You have been offered a good job in another city, but you don't really want to live there.

2. You are fired from your job without a reason.

3. You were told that you would get a raise after six months, but the raise hasn't come through.

4. Your boss is very difficult to get along with.

5. You think you are being discriminated against in your job because of your race, religion, or gender.

6. No one calls you back after a job interview.

7. An employer offers you a job for which you know you are not qualified.

8. Someone in your department gets a promotion, and you think you are better qualified for that job.

9. You're having trouble getting along with a new co-worker.

10. You are told you have to work overtime, but you can't because you have young children.

11. You are unhappy at your job, but there are not many openings in your field.

12. You are asked to do personal chores for your boss that you feel are not part of your job.

13. You find out that your co-workers go out together regularly after work, and you are not included.

14. You are invited to your boss's house for dinner and you don't know what to wear or bring.

15. You are bored with your job and want to try something new, but don't know where to start.

THE JOB INTERVIEW

LISTENING ACTIVITY 10

    C   Practise the conversation with a partner.

Interviewer:	Hello, Barbara. Please come in.
Barbara:	Thank you.
Interviewer:	Let's see, you're applying for the job in the marketing department, is that right?
Barbara:	Yes, that's correct.
Interviewer:	Do you have any experience in marketing?
Barbara:	Yes, I worked in the advertising department of a large store in Toronto.
Interviewer:	I see. How long did you work there?
Barbara:	For three years.
Interviewer:	Do you have any other related experience?

Barbara: Yes, I worked part-time in a clothing store while I was in college. That was for about two years.

Interviewer: Why did you leave your last job?

Barbara: I left because my husband got a job here, in Vancouver. We moved here two months ago.

Interviewer: Can you tell me about your education?

Barbara: Yes, I have a college degree in business. I specialized in marketing.

Interviewer: Can you tell me a little about yourself, your strengths and weaknesses.

Barbara: Well, I'm a "people-person." I love to work with people, and I'm also creative. I like working in sales and marketing.

Interviewer: I see. Well, you seem to be well qualified for this job. Do you have any questions you'd like to ask?

Barbara: Yes, I do. I know about the products your company sells, but I'd like to know a little more about the specific job I'd be hired for.

Interviewer: You'd be working in a team, preparing advertisements for our stores in western Canada. The job is full-time. This is a big company, so there are opportunities for promotion in the future.

Barbara: That sounds very interesting.

Interviewer: We have several people to interview this week, but we'll call you by the end of next week if we are interested in hiring you.

Barbara: Thank you very much.

Community Contact Task 1

1. Work in a group. Decide on three different things you want more information about. Suitable examples include finding a dentist, an arena in your neighbourhood, a place to repair an appliance.

2. Look up the subjects in the Yellow Pages directory.

    a) How many places are listed for each subject? (If many, how many pages?)

    b) Which of the ads do you find most informative?

    c) Which features does the ad have?

    - colour

    - pictures

    - information about how long the company has been in business

3. Would you choose to go to any of the places you see advertised? Why or why not?

4. Compare the ads for the three different products you chose. How similar or different are the ads?

Community Contact Task 2

1. Go to a grocery store. Look for the following items. On the worksheet, circle the containers that these foods come in.

Soup	Cookies	Fruit juice	Cheese
box	box	can	wooden box
can	paper bag	jar	plastic container
jar	cellophane wrapped	carton	wrapped in plastic
envelope	cardboard container (if frozen)	plastic bottle	wrapped in paper
plastic container (if frozen)		drinking box	on a styrofoam tray

Add one item of your own, and list the containers it comes in.

2. List all the containers that are easy to recycle.

3. List all the containers that are difficult to recycle.

4. How can you carry these items home from the store you visit?

   a) in a plastic bag

   b) in a paper bag

   c) in a cloth bag

5. Did you bring your own bag?

Community Contact Task 3

In Class

Work with a partner. Name five places you can buy snack food.

In the Community

With your partner, go to one of the places and complete the chart. Use the worksheet.

	Kinds	Sizes	Prices	Calories (if listed)
a chocolate bar				
a granola bar				
potato chips				
peanuts				
popcorn				
a muffin				
cookies				
a doughnut				
a bagel				

Choose three products. Eat them and describe them.

Reporting Back

Work in a group. Share your information.

Community Contact Task 4

In Class

Work in a group. Predict the answers to these questions.

Winterizing cars:

1. What products are used?

2. Where are the products bought?

3. What services are needed? (For example, changing the tires)

4. Who does the work?

Winterizing houses:

1. What changes are made to doors, windows, etc.?

2. What products are bought? (salt, etc.)

In the Community

Do a survey. Ask three people in the community these questions about how they prepare for winter.

Reporting Back

Work in a group. Compare your information. Make a list of the most common things that people do.

Community Contact Task 5

In the Community

Work in pairs. Do a survey. Ask five people outside of class the following questions:

1. Have you ever taken a day off work or class when you were not really sick?

2. If so, what were the real reasons?

3. What excuse did you give your boss or teacher?

4. What is the best excuse you ever used, or heard someone use, for taking a day off?

Reporting Back

Work in groups. Share your information. Make a list of the most unusual excuses from each group.

Community Contact Task 6

In the Community

Work in pairs. Do a survey. Ask five people outside of class the following questions:

1. How often do you line up to wait for something?

2. What kinds of things are you willing to wait for? (Example: tickets to a show you want to see)

3. What kinds of things would you not wait in line for?

4. What is the longest you would wait for something that is important to you?

5. What is the longest you would wait on the telephone if someone put you on hold?

Reporting Back

Work in groups. Share your information.

Community Contact Task 7

In the Community

Go to a bank. Find out the following:

1. What kind of bank accounts are available?

2. How do you get a bank card?

3. What services can you get with a bank card?

4. How many banking machines are there at the bank?

5. What hours are the bank open?

6. What hours are the banking machines available?

7. What is the service charge for transactions on the banking machine?

8. What are the service charges for going to the teller?

Reporting Back

Work in groups. Discuss what you found. Which banks have the best deals?

Community Contact Task 8

In Class

Work in a group. Make a list of jobs that interest you. Discuss where you could find information about these jobs.

In the Community

Work with a partner. Go to a Canada Employment Centre. Ask questions to find out about jobs that are available and qualifications needed for these jobs.

Reporting Back

Work in a group. Discuss your information.

Appendix 1: Spelling

Spelling Verb Forms Ending "ing"

The spelling rules for continuous verbs are different from the rules for regular past tense verbs. For example, with the verb **try**, the past tense is **tried**, but the continuous tense is **trying**.

Rule 1   Verbs that end with **e** drop the e and add **ing**:

write   writing

Rule 2   Verbs that end with two consonants or with two vowels plus one consonant add **ing**:

help   helping
read   reading

Rule 3   Verbs that end with a vowel and a consonant double the final letter and add **ing**:

run   running

Exceptions: consonants **w**, **x**, and **y**. (**buy**   **buying**)

Note: Verbs that end in **ie** change the **ie** to **y** and add **ing**:

die   dying
lie   lying

Spelling Simple Past Tense

2 consonants	add **ed**	work	work**ed**
2 vowels + consonant	add **ed**	need	need**ed**
vowel + **y**	add **ed**	play	play**ed**
consonant + **y**	change **y** to **i** add **ed**	try	tri**ed**
vowel + consonant	double consonant add **ed**	plan	plan**ned**

Not all verbs that end in vowel + consonant double the final letter. Common exceptions are **listened**, **opened**, **answered**.

Spelling Rules with Comparative Forms

Adjectives that end in **y** change **y** to **i** and add **er** for the comparative or **est** for the superlative form:

happy   happier
silly   silliest

Adjectives that end in vowel + consonant double the final letter and add **er** for the comparative or **est** for the superlative form:

fat	fatter
thin	thinnest

Spelling Plural Nouns

Nouns that end in **s**, **ch**, **sh**, **z**, **o**, **x** add **es** to form the plural:

watch	watches
box	boxes
potato	potatoes

Nouns that end in consonant + **y** change the **y** to **i** and add **es** for the plural form:

city	cities
activity	activities

Nouns that end in vowel + **y** add **s**:

day	days
key	keys

Nouns that end in **f** or **fe** change the **f** to **v** and add **es** to form the plural:

leaf	leaves
knife	knives

Irregular Plurals

person	people
child	children
woman	women
man	men
mouse	mice
foot	feet
tooth	teeth
ox	oxen

Appendix 2: Irregular Verbs

Many past participles are the same as the regular or irregular past tense forms. Irregular past participles are shown in bold type below.

Present	Past	Past participle
arise	arose	**arisen**
awake	awoke	**awaken**
be	was, were	**been**
beat	beat	**beaten**
become	became	**become**
begin	began	**begun**
bite	bit	**bitten**
bleed	bled	bled
blow	blew	**blown**
break	broke	**broken**
bring	brought	brought
build	built	built
buy	bought	bought
catch	caught	caught
choose	chose	**chosen**
come	came	**come**
cost	cost	cost
cut	cut	cut
dig	dug	dug
do	did	**done**
draw	drew	**drawn**
drink	drank	**drunk**
drive	drove	**driven**
eat	ate	**eaten**
fall	fell	**fallen**
feed	fed	fed
feel	felt	felt
find	found	found
fly	flew	**flown**
forbid	forbade	**forbidden**
forget	forgot	**forgotten**
forgive	forgave	**forgiven**
freeze	froze	**frozen**
get	got	**gotten** (got)
give	gave	**given**
go	went	**gone**
grow	grew	**grown**
have	had	had
hear	heard	heard
hide	hid	**hidden**
hit	hit	hit

Present	Past	Past participle
hold	held	held
hurt	hurt	hurt
keep	kept	kept
know	knew	**known**
lay	laid	laid
lead	led	led
leave	left	left
let	let	let
lie	lay	**lain**
lose	lost	lost
make	made	made
mean	meant	meant
meet	met	met
pay	paid	paid
put	put	put
read	read	read
ride	rode	**ridden**
ring	rang	**rung**
rise	rose	**risen**
run	ran	**ran**
see	saw	**seen**
sell	sold	sold
send	sent	sent
shake	shook	**shaken**
shine	shone	shone
shoot	shot	shot
show	showed	shown
shrink	shrank	**shrunk**
shut	shut	shut
sing	sang	**sung**
sit	sat	sat
sleep	slept	slept
speak	spoke	**spoken**
spread	spread	spread
spring	sprang	**sprung**
stand	stood	stood
steal	stole	**stolen**
stink	stank	**stunk**
swear	swore	**sworn**
swim	swam	**swum**
take	took	taken
teach	taught	taught
tear	tore	**torn**
tell	told	told
think	thought	thought
throw	threw	**thrown**
understand	understood	understood
wake	woke	**woken**
wear	wore	**worn**
win	won	won
write	wrote	**written**

Englisch ist einfach

ben englizce oranmak stiurum

私は英語が好きです。

بی أحب هذا الكتاب

Vaya suka buku ini

Bu Kitapi cok scudim

我
會
説
英
文

See you in Canadian Concepts 5!

Delam mikhad englisi yad begiram

এটা আমার   Mi piace molto questo
libro

Tôi thích quyển sách này

Inglês é fácil de aprender.

Je parle l'anglais

안녕

私はこの本が大好きです。

Μιλαω Eλληνικά

ME GUSTA HABLAR INGLES

Μου αρέσει αυτό το Βιβλίο